MW01135875

UNREASONABLE INFERENCES

*The True Story of a Wrongful Conviction
and Its Astonishing Aftermath*

Michael Griesbach

Published by Point Beach Publishing, LLC

Grateful acknowledgment is recognized to the *Milwaukee Journal Sentinel* and to the Associated Press for permission to reprint the following photographs that appear in this book: courtesy of the *Journal Sentinel* for the photo depicting Steven Avery at the Avery Salvage Yard and for the photo of Steven Avery being escorted to court; and courtesy of the Associated Press for the photo of the candle light vigil for Teresa Halbach.

ISBN – 978-0-578-06957-9

PRINTED IN THE
UNITED STATES OF AMERICA

To Mom and Dad, for everything

Acknowledgements

They say anyone can write a book if they have something to say, and I'm living proof that it's true. But you can't write a book alone without losing your mind and I have many people to thank for keeping mine somewhat intact.

Thanks first to my editor, Andrew Loduha. Your enthusiasm and support, your knack for getting it just right, and your knowledge of all things relating to books were indispensible. Our working breakfasts at Four Seasons and countless e-mails were always productive and never a chore. It was a privilege to work with you.

Thanks to Jody, Mary, Perry, Dan, Erik, Kerry, and mom. Reviewing early versions of manuscripts is an unenviable task, but you did it with good cheer. Your advice was always sound and your encouragement is what kept me going.

Thanks to Keith Findley at the Wisconsin Innocence Project and distinguished professor Janine Geske at Marquette University's law school. From when we first learned about the DNA until today, I've treasured our conversations.

Thanks to Steve Glynn, Walt Kelly and Ron Kaminski – for your wise counsel and moral support. Your commitment to justice is inspiring.

Thanks to Penny Beerntsen, whose courage and compassion turned what could have been a life-long tragedy into a mission to serve. As a member of the Wisconsin Criminal Justice Study Commission and the Wisconsin Crime Victims Rights Board in the years following her assault, and as a volunteer for the Manitowoc County Sexual Assault Resource Center, the Wisconsin Department of Corrections Restorative Justice Program, and Northwestern University law school's Innocence Project, Penny has devoted much of her time and considerable talent to helping crime victims and offenders alike get their lives back on track. Her life is an inspiration.

Thanks to William Zinsser, whose classic book, *On Writing Well*, about the craft of writing creative non-fiction, helped immeasurably – I marked up more of his book than I left alone.

Thanks to Jared Guzman. Your public relations savvy and your timely marketing advice were indispensible to this endeavor's success.

Thanks to the servers at Manitowoc Coffee, Starbucks, and the Golden Flame – your hospitality and bottomless cups of coffee kept me going when I wanted to quit.

Thanks to Manitowoc County District Attorney Mark Rohrer, who fosters an office where the number one duty is to try our best to do what's right.

And most of all, thanks to Jody and the kids for your love and support. You have put up with an often absent husband and dad for two and a half years but while it may sound trite, it's true – I couldn't have done it without you.

Prologue

Nature's beauty comes not from the spectacular in East Central Wisconsin. There are no thousand foot vertical drop-off cliffs, like at Yosemite, or million cubic feet per second waterfalls, like at Niagara. No, the land here owes its beauty to its moderation, its balance, its order. In between the extremes of the monolithic vistas of the Great Plains on the one hand, and the confining woods of New England on the other, the land here seems just right somehow.

But our climate is anything but moderate, and it's from our climate that we're reminded how fragile life can be. Most meteorologists say it's a myth, but some claim Lake Michigan protects East Central Wisconsin from the deadliest of summer storms. The Great Lake's frigid water cools the atmosphere, they say, and robs the beastly storms of the warm, moist air they feed on for their strength.

Perhaps there's something to it, but twice in the not so distant past the darker side of Mother Nature ignored Lake Michigan and brewed up storms so powerful that they shattered the balance of the atmosphere and laid waste to parts of the land. This book, in a manner of speaking, is the story of those two storms. The first storm shattered the glass on the courthouse dome, and the second one nearly left the local justice system in ruins.

INTRODUCTION

I've been a prosecutor for twenty-two years and I thought I'd seen it all. I've been called out to crime scenes in the middle of the night to view victims with gunshot or stab wounds lying mangled in pools of congealing blood. I've comforted overwrought rape victims paralyzed by fear so they could muster up the courage to take the stand. I've interviewed victims of armed robberies who stared death in the eyes and know they are lucky to still be alive. And one time, I even saw tough-guy cops with tears in their eyes and fear on their faces as they scrambled into the night to find the two young hoodlums who shot and killed one of their own.

I've sat almost comatose through thousands of hours of mindless Intake Court, listening to the pleas of defendants, "not guilty, Your Honor," ceremoniously uttered over and over. I've seen my fair share of pompous prosecutors, joined battle with belligerent defense attorneys, and paced courthouse hallways late at night, sweating it out while waiting for a verdict.

But none of that prepared me for the case you're about to read, a true crime story where the good guys are sometimes the bad guys and the bad guys the good. It's a case of violent crime with a mind-numbing twist. But mostly, it's a case about innocence and guilt.

PART I

ONE

July 14, 1985

IT WAS IMPOSSIBLE to identify him. With the exception of her one-piece bathing suit that had been hanging on the clothesline, but was now wrapped around his head, the intruder was nude. The seventeen year old girl thought for a moment she was dreaming, but the knife the man held to her throat was real. This wasn't a dream.

"Say anything and I'll kill you," said the man, sitting on top of her with one hand over her mouth and the other on her breast.

"Take off your clothes," he demanded, "Take off your clothes, or I'll kill you."

The girl pointed to the heating pad underneath her and blurted out she was having her period. The man felt the heating pad and then placed the girl's hand on his penis as she squirmed in disgust.

Then he yanked her off the bed, and with the knife to her throat again, he took her by the arm and pushed her to the back door.

"Call anyone, and I'll come back and kill you," said the man, as he ran into the darkness, leaving as he entered – nude.

For the police, determining the point of entry proved easy. The intruder had dragged a picnic table underneath the kitchen window, popped open the flimsy screen, and let himself in. They had a suspect in mind, but it was too dark for the girl to get a good look at the man; he was around 5'8" with a solid build, possibly a beard, but that's all she knew. So the investigation led nowhere. There was a predator on the loose, and the police knew he'd strike again – the only question was when.

Two weeks later

Like most afternoons during the past few weeks, on July 29, 1985, Tom and Penny Beerntsen went to the beach. The Beerntsens made their home in Manitowoc, Wisconsin – a city of thirty-eight thousand on the western shore of Lake Michigan, seventy miles north of Milwaukee and thirty miles south of Green Bay. A stone's throw from the hallowed grounds of Lambeau field, the citizens of Manitowoc, whose moods rise and fall with the fortunes of their beloved Packers, are proud to be called cheeseheads.

The couple owned and operated Beerntsen's Confectionary on North Eighth Street in the heart of Manitowoc's historic downtown. To step into Beerntsen's is to step into the past. Tom's grandparents opened the old fashioned candy store and ice cream parlor in 1932, and Tom and Penny were its current caretakers. With home-made chocolates and candies artfully displayed behind glass paned counters and elegant black walnut booths gracing the parlor, Beerntsen's Confectionary is one of Manitowoc's jewels.

Tom and Penny both grew up in Manitowoc. They met in seventh grade and began dating during their sophomore year in high school. Together, they attended a small liberal arts school in Downers Grove, Illinois and were married during their third year there. They graduated in 1971, Tom with a Bachelor of Science in Applied Behavioral Science, and Penny with a Bachelor of Arts in Sociology. They spent the first dozen years of their marriage moving from one state to the next – from Illinois to Iowa, then to South Dakota, and later to Minnesota, as Tom accepted various positions at regional YMCAs throughout the Midwest, eventually attaining the position of CEO. Penny raised their two children, a daughter and then a son. She also worked as a physical fitness instructor and later on as a staff member at a mental health center across the Iowa border in Illinois. Having been on the move for more than a decade, and longing for a more permanent place to call home, they moved back to Manitowoc in 1983 to run Tom's parents' candy store.

Now it was two years later and, as usual, it took a long time for summer to arrive that year on "the Lakeshore" – as the local television and radio personalities call east-central Wisconsin, even if nobody else does. And as usual, Lake Michigan was the culprit. For months, forecasters had qualified their predictions of a warm up with the worn-out phrase, "cooler near the lake," and the patience of local residents wore thin. But someone flipped the switch in mid-June and the prevailing northeasterly winds mercifully ceased.

With summer now in full swing, the Beerntsens frequently spent late afternoons on the beach at Neshotah Park, a fifteen minute drive from Manitowoc just north of Two Rivers. In addition to raising the kids and running the confectionary with Tom, Penny was the physical fitness instructor at the YMCA, and now that her summer fitness class was underway, she exercised religiously. A six mile run, often along the Lake Michigan shoreline, anchored her daily routine.

That Monday was a perfect day for the beach, and with their ten-year-old -daughter and eight-year-old son, Tom and Penny planned to take full advantage of it. Tom pulled their Dodge Caravan into the parking lot and then grabbed the cooler while Penny scoped out the beach for a place to set up camp. With sunshine and a mild breeze off the lake, the quarter mile stretch of beach was packed with sunbathers, but Penny found a spot at the edge of the sand and popped open an oversized umbrella to protect them from the sun. She read a few pages from the summer novel she'd been at since school let out while Tom kept an eye on the kids who splashed around in the fifty five degree water.

Penny would testify months later that it was precisely three o'clock that afternoon when she removed her red and white striped tee shirt and got ready for her run. She knew it was three because a few days earlier she'd struggled against a strong headwind, and Tom and the kids were worried when she was late getting back to the park. This time, she wanted to make sure she was back in an hour, so she checked her watch before leaving – three o'clock on the nose. She said goodbye to Tom and then started jogging north along the smooth wet sand at the edge of the water – barefoot in her bikini.

Penny jogged past the edge of the park and crossed into a state forest a few minutes later. Lying immediately to the north of Neshotah Park, Point Beach State Forest transforms Lake Michigan's shoreline into an isolated wilderness. Undulating rows of sand dunes run like waves parallel to the shore and hide from view whatever occurs in their troughs. Towering pines rise sixty feet into the sky at the edge of the forest fifty yards inland and stand guard with an ever watchful and imposing eye over the beach below.

A mile and a half into her run now, Penny gazed out at the sparkling waters of Lake Michigan to her right and the deep forest of Point Beach to her left. With awe, not fear, a sense of utter isolation filtered into her psyche. Bathed in sunlight, with endorphins surging, she felt like she was on top of the world.

She had passed the scraggly-looking man just beyond the public area of the beach fifteen minutes earlier, and despite temperatures in the mid-eighties, the man had a leather jacket on. Kind of odd given the temperature, she thought to herself.

"Nice day for a jog," the man had said.

"Yes, it's a beautiful day," Penny replied over her left shoulder as she jogged past.

But that was fifteen minutes ago, and Penny wasn't about to let the strange-looking man put a damper on her run. She crossed "First Creek," as the locals call the shallow stream that empties into Lake Michigan there, and a half mile further she spied a sailboat running on its auxiliary motor with its sails down. The small craft was traveling in the same direction as she was, so she made a game out of jogging at the same pace.

By the time she crossed "Second Creek" a mile further north she had found her stride and had worked up a considerable sweat. At the halfway point of her run now, she checked her watch as she made the turn and headed back toward the park. Perfect – three-thirty, right on schedule.

She spotted the odd-looking man again twenty minutes later. He'd walked a half mile further north, well into the wilderness now, and he was standing in the midst of a stubby poplar tree ten feet from the water and fifty yards ahead of her. At first, she wasn't afraid – just curious. Why had the man walked so far up the beach with his street clothes on? And why was he hiding in the midst of a poplar tree just thirty feet in front of her now?

A few strides later, she noticed that the man's face looked different this time. It wasn't the odd, but seemingly harmless face of the stranger that she'd come across earlier. No, the man looked determined this time, determined to do something terrible – and he wasn't even trying to hide it. Penny's curiosity rapidly turned to fear. She knew she was in trouble. Each second stretched into what seemed like forever, and her heart began to pound. She didn't change her pace as she approached the man, and she didn't look him in the eye. Maybe he wouldn't do anything if she ignored him – maybe he wouldn't be real somehow.

But the man in the midst of the poplar tree wasn't just her imagination – he was less than ten feet in front of her now. Penny angled into the water. The man lunged at her, but missed. She angled a little further out and considered diving into the deeper water, but she was afraid he'd swim after her and she'd drown in a struggle. It was difficult to run in the waist deep water and the man was gaining on her, so Penny arched back toward the shore. But she didn't have a chance. The attacker lunged at her from behind and wrapped his arms around her upper body. She tried twisting free, but the man placed her in a bear hug and dragged her to the shore.

"Help, Help!" Penny yelled to a sailboat two hundred yards from shore.

But the man tightened his grip and cut off her windpipe. "Shut up," he grunted, "we're gonna take a little walk up the sand."

With his prey onshore now, the attacker started pushing Penny over the first dune. She dug her feet into the sand and pushed back as hard as she could, but at five feet two and 105 pounds, the man easily overpowered her and manhandled her over the dunes, ripping off her bikini top along the way.

He loosened his grip for a few seconds and Penny almost twisted free, but then he squeezed even harder and dragged her to the edge of the woods. Fifty yards from the beach now, and concealed from view, the assailant had Penny exactly where he wanted her.

He ripped off his belt, unsnapped his jeans, and exposed his erect penis. Then he pushed Penny a little further into the woods and pulled off her bikini bottoms. Face to face for the first time, she got a good look at the man, but he was bearded and it was difficult to make out his facial features.

"Do what I tell you," he mumbled, "I have a knife."

He began fondling Penny's breasts and then he sucked on her right breast, biting her slightly.

"Make me hard," he demanded.

Somehow, Penny kept her wits about her and tried reasoning with the man: "I've been gone too long. My husband will be worried and he'll come looking for me."

But the man didn't buy it: "Make me hard," he demanded again.

Penny yelled back in anger and disgust: "No!"

Then he reminded her about the knife, and Penny reluctantly placed her hand on his penis while she squirmed in disgust.

"Play with yourself," he said, while he fondled her.

Penny removed her hand from his penis and put it on herself.

"Now put your mouth on my penis."

"No!" Penny shot back.

"Put your fucking mouth on my penis, you're really fucking this up."

Penny refused again and then the assailant shoved her to the ground. Anger spewed viciously from his filthy mouth: "Spread your legs. Spread your god-damned legs. You're fucking this up."

Penny held fast.

And then, he beat her. She heard a crack as he jerked her nose to the side, and then he pummeled her face with relentless blows to her eyes, nose, cheeks, and forehead. She kicked him in the groin, but he grabbed her around her neck and began strangling her like a madman.

"Now you're gonna die, bitch."

He shook her so violently that her head pounded up and down against the ground, and she thought any second he'd bring out the knife and stab her to death in the sand.

Penny was close to passing out, but the man wanted her alive so he loosened his grip and screamed at her: "Now, are you going to do it or not?"

"Okay, I'll do it," Penny said softly, trying to buy time, "but I'm sure my husband is looking for me. I've been gone too long."

That infuriated him, and the beating resumed until a few minutes later when Penny looked up and saw him inexplicably scramble away and miraculously disappear into the woods.

But the attack had taken its toll. Naked, bloodied, and badly bruised, Penny was barely able to move. She rolled onto her hands and knees and tried to get up, but she immediately fell down. Desperate to get into the open where someone could see her, she started crawling instead, but half way to the water she was too weak to go on. Empty, devoid of emotion, she sat cross legged and stared blankly into the sparkling waters of Lake Michigan – alone among the towering pines. She looked down at her hands and wondered where all the blood came from, and then she gave up for the moment and lay on her back in the sand.

When she came to, Penny summoned up all the energy she could and resumed crawling toward the water. After twenty minutes she finally made it, and then she began washing the blood off her face – the last thing she wanted was for her children to see her like that, all beaten and bloody. Then she saw a young couple walking on the beach. "Help, help," Penny shouted, as she curled up into a ball to hide her nakedness. The woman ran over and wrapped a towel around her, and with Penny in the middle, the three of them began walking down the beach toward Neshotah Park.

Penny saw a man approaching – it was Tom!

Location of Assault

Tom Beerntsen bolted toward his wife and lifted her into his arms. "Oh, my God, what happened?"

"A man tried raping me, Tom, he tried to kill me! Where's Julie?"

"Don't worry, she's with her grandfather."

"What about Mike?"

"My mom's taking care of it. Don't worry, honey."

Tom Beerntsen ran down the beach with his wife in his arms. An ambulance was waiting when they made it back to the parking lot, and the EMTs lifted her inside and rushed her to Memorial Hospital in Manitowoc – sirens wailing.

Penny was safe now. Whoever he was, the man who attacked her had chosen the wrong victim. She had kicked and clawed and screamed at him relentlessly, and with his victim showing no sign of surrender, it was the would-be rapist, not the victim, who paradoxically gave in.

TWO

ON JULY 23, 1985, six days before Penny Beerntsen was assaulted by a madman on the Lake Michigan shoreline, Lori Avery gave birth to a pair of healthy baby boys. Memorial Hospital in Manitowoc had granted her a five day stay because birth of the twins was by C Section, qualifying her pregnancy as "complicated." Besides, it was 1985, and early release for the uninsured was not yet standard operating procedure.

Choosing names for the boys hadn't been easy. After all, most new parents have a difficult time coming up with one name – let alone two. Maybe Lori and her husband Steve didn't know that Billy is a nickname for William; maybe they didn't know that tacking "Jr." at the end of a boy's name means his name is the same as his dad's; or maybe they knew both, but just didn't care. But whatever the reason, the names Steve and Lori chose for their two baby boys were William and Billy Jr.

The Averys had three other children, each, thankfully with a separate and distinct name. Another boy, at four, was the oldest and two girls, ages one and two, rounded off the family.

On the night Lori was released from the hospital, she and Steve went to the stock car races at the Highway 141 Speedway. It was a celebration of sorts for the birth of William and Billy, Jr. It was also an Enduro race, and Steve wouldn't miss one of those for the world. The cars in an Enduro race are stripped to the bone. All the glass except the windshield is removed, and only the driver's seat is left inside. Steve had a blast watching the old wrecks crash into each other as they raced around the dirt track. Lori was happy too. She was excited about the newborns, and so was Steve. Lord knows, he'd put her through enough over the years, but since the incident last January he seemed to have changed – or at least he was trying.

It started in late November. Sandy Murphy, the wife of Manitowoc County reserve deputy Bill Murphy, lived right up the road from the Averys, and she had to drive past their house on her way to work at five-thirty a.m. Steve would get up early, grab his field glasses, and peer down the road to see when Sandy was leaving. Then he'd wait for her to drive past, and depending on how screwed up he was that day, he'd either rub himself on the hood of his truck or jump out into the road, nude. Sandy nearly struck him one time.

The most serious incident happened about seven months ago, on January 3, 1985. Sandy pulled out of her driveway at the usual time and started driving down the road past Steve and Lori's. She had her six-month-old baby in the car that morning, and she planned to drop him off at her parents' house in town. Just past the Avery residence she looked in her rearview mirror and saw lights approaching from behind. The truck seemed to come out of nowhere. It began passing on her left, and then without warning it rammed into the side of her car. Sandy careened back and forth, but somehow she managed to maintain control of her car.

Sandy pulled over to the side of the road to inspect the damage, but before getting out of her car she looked up and saw Steven Avery walking toward her. He was pointing a rifle at her head. He ordered her to get into his truck, but Sandy motioned to the back seat and told him her baby would freeze to death if she left him alone. Avery looked inside the car and told her she could go.

Steve had committed plenty of serious crimes over the years, but accosting the wife of a deputy sheriff on the road that morning was one of the dumbest. Sandy Murphy knew him – they were practically neighbors for crying out loud – and she called the police immediately to report the crime.

Three deputies arrested him within the hour, and when they searched his house, they found a .30-06 rifle stashed under one of the kids' beds with a live round in the chamber. Steve even confessed. Yes, he rammed his Blazer into Mrs. Murphy' car. Yes, he pointed the gun at her. And yes, he planned to force her into his truck.

The D.A. threw the book at him, charging him with two counts of endangering safety by conduct evincing a depraved mind – one count for the mother and one for her child – and one count of felon in possession of a firearm. By virtue of his two prior convictions, Steve was an "habitual offender," so the prosecutor dutifully tacked on the appropriate penalty enhancer, which increased the maximum sentence on each count by six years. He faced a maximum sentence of forty-eight years in prison, but for some reason bail was set at only two thousand dollars, which Steve's mom and dad posted forthwith. He was a free man pending trial.

* * *

Seven months had passed since the incident with Sandy Murphy, and now it was the morning after the Enduro race – the same day that Penny Beerntsen was assaulted on the beach fifteen miles east of the Avery Salvage Yard. Lori got up early, but Steve drank more than he should have the night before, and he was still in bed at quarter to nine when she told him to get up and start helping out. They had lots of errands to run and it was time to get moving.

Lori had the kids fed, dressed, and ready to go within half an hour and when Steve was ready, they piled the kids into his 1976 Chevy Blazer and headed into town. First stop was Fleet Farm, where Steve bought a five gallon pail of plaster to repair some cracks in the living room ceiling. According to a receipt received into evidence five months later, the cost of the plaster was $8.29.

Next was Shopko, where exterior paint was supposed to be on sale for $8.99 a gallon. Lori had started to paint the house in mid-June, but she wisely put the project on hold when her due date got closer. The last thing she needed was to fall off a ladder. Steve went into Shopko while Lori stayed back in the car with the kids, but the sale was off, and as Steve would later testify, "They sure as hell weren't gonna pay $17.99 for a gallon of paint."

Then they drove up the shore to Two Rivers, or "Trivers," as those of us who live here pronounce it, where they stopped at Wolfe-Snyder Drug Store to fill a prescription for Lori. This time Steve stayed back with the kids while Lori went inside. On her way out, Lori remembered they were running low on milk so she ducked into the Red Owl grocery store next door and picked up a few gallons. The sun was getting hotter by the hour, and with five fidgety kids all under four years old in a truck without air-conditioning, it was time to go home. Steve wanted to stop at his mom and dad's place on

14

the way home, and Lori agreed, not that she had much of a choice.

Allan and Dolores Avery lived on forty acres of scrabble land out on Highway 147, about twelve miles north of Manitowoc. In addition to their home, the property is also the site of the family business – the Avery Salvage Yard – which turned a decent profit back then, and still does today.

Steve's mom pulled into the gravel driveway right behind them and asked Steve if he could help his dad pour a few slabs of concrete – they had a big project going and could sure use the help if he and Lori had the time. As Steve put it later, they "didn't have nothin' to do that day" so he was glad to pitch in.

For Lori, a long morning of running errands in town turned into a long afternoon of visiting family at the Salvage Yard. Steve's Aunt Rose and his sister Barb were already there, and more family and a few friends of the family arrived as the day wore on. Lori persevered, keeping an eye on the kids and occasionally visiting with her in-laws while Steve went outside.

Allan Avery was putting up a sheep shed. The idea was to graze sheep in the hilly acres of the junk yard to keep the grass from getting too tall around the cars. He already had the sheep and now he needed some sheds, so he had ordered a load of cement that day for the foundation.

Steve shot the bull with his brother, Chuck, and the rest of the guys until the cement truck turned off Avery Road and pulled into the driveway a few minutes later. When the truck couldn't squeeze through the gate, he hopped into a wrecker and hauled a couple junked cars out of the way. Then the truck backed into position in front of the foundation for the first shed, and the driver lowered the chute. Steve directed the chute so the cement poured evenly while the other guys spread it around with shovels, and after that, the whole crew went over and poured a second slab for another shed. Steve and Chuck filled a wheelbarrow with the last of the cement and poured a small slab that their dad wanted in front of the garage, throwing in some loose gravel so the cement would rise to the top – not a bad way to stretch a load of cement if you're running thin.

With the entire job completed, Steve went inside to tell Lori to get the kids ready – it was time to go home. Lori took longer than she should have to say her goodbyes, and when she went outside she couldn't find Steve. She was exhausted, and she wanted to go home. Why would he disappear like that? He knew she'd been caring for William and Billy Jr. non-stop since the moment they were born six days earlier, not to mention the three older kids, who constantly vied for her attention and needed her now more than ever. Sometimes it seemed like he just didn't care, Lori thought to herself, and she was getting sick of it.

It was 4:30 – thirty minutes after Penny Beerntsen was assaulted – when Steve finally came back up to the house and said they should get going. Steve later told the police he had taken his sister for a ride down at the quarry on his brand new four-wheeler, though he didn't tell Lori where he was until even later. They said their goodbyes to Steve's parents and headed out in the Blazer, leaving a trail of dust as they sped down Avery Road.

Lori assumed they were going home, but a few miles down the road Steve said they were going out to eat at R&M's instead, a little burger joint just over the county line. Five minutes later, he changed his mind. Now he wanted to drive all the way up to Green Bay to see if the ShopKo there still had the damned paint on sale.

They arrived in Green Bay a half hour later, and with five hungry kids crammed into the back seat of the Chevy Blazer, their first stop was the drive-through at Burger-King.

After that, Steve pulled into a car wash across the street. The Blazer was covered in mud, and Steve wanted to hose it down before they drove home.

When they got to ShopKo Steve went to the paint section while Lori took one of the girls to the bathroom. It looked like the sale was over, but Steve checked every can in case they left a price tag on one. No luck. But Lori talked him into buying the paint anyhow. Despite the progress she made before the twins were born, there was still a good chunk of the house left to paint and Lori was determined to get it done that summer. So they grabbed a gallon and proceeded to the checkout lane where they were given a receipt that later established the precise time they were in Green Bay. It was 5:13 p.m., an hour and fifteen minutes after Penny Beerntsen was attacked on the beach nearly thirty miles away.

After they left ShopKo, Steve dragged them to an automotive store on Green Bay's west side where he looked at truck accessories for awhile. And finally, after stopping at another drive-through – Hardee's this time – they headed back home.

THREE

THE STAFF WAS waiting when the EMTs rushed Penny into the emergency room at Memorial Hospital. The attacker had pummeled her face, and the ER doctor on duty enumerated her wounds: severe bruising and swelling around both eyes; bleeding inside the right eye with a deep cut underneath that took several stitches to close; a fractured nose; scattered bruises on her back and a more pronounced bruise at the base of her neck; and shattered fingernails on her right hand from clawing at her assailant.

Deputy Judy Dvorak was the first officer to respond to the hospital. Following procedure, she started interviewing Penny even before the nurses were finished treating her wounds. Still shaking and struggling to see out of her nearly swollen shut eyes, Penny told Deputy Dvorak how the man with the leather jacket grabbed her while she was jogging down the beach, how he man-handled her over the dunes, and then pushed her into the woods where he viciously assaulted her.

Manitowoc County Sheriff Tom Kocourek arrived twenty minutes later. The Kocoureks and the Beerntsens knew each other – they attended the same church and were practically neighbors. So the Sheriff joined Tom Beerntsen in the emergency room lobby and offered him what little comfort he could.

Kocourek started his career as a patrol officer, and later a detective with the Manitowoc Police Department before moving over to the Sheriff's Department in 1977, where he steadily moved up the ranks. Elected in 1979, he had to run for office every two years, but Kocourek never faced serious political opposition. He was a man of law and order, the kind of man voters trusted, and every two years the citizens of Manitowoc County rewarded him with another term.

The Sheriff's large rimmed rectangular glasses and neatly combed gray hair exuded intelligence and a no-nonsense competence that people admired. He rarely smiled, and when he did, it was a thin expressionless smile. To some he came off as aloof, but to all he was known as a straight shooter – when Tom Kocourek said something, you could take it to the bank.

He assured Tom he'd do everything in his power to bring Penny's assailant to justice. Manitowoc County doesn't allow this sort of thing to happen, especially to people like the Beerntsens, and his department wouldn't rest until they apprehended the reprobate who was responsible.

Looking back, it would have been better if Kocourek had backed off and let his detectives handle the investigation instead. As the administrator of one of the largest agency's budget in the County, he didn't have time to involve himself in criminal investigations. But he called the shots in this one. Mostly, though, it was his personal acquaintance with the Beerntsens that should have disqualified him. Years later, a private investigator recalled that in all the years he practiced his trade in Manitowoc County, he never saw Sheriff Kocourek investigate another crime. Not once.

The Sheriff joined Deputy Dvorak in the emergency room and listened carefully as she wrapped up her interview of Penny. Although he had to step out of the room during the medical examination, he did ask Penny a few questions – especially about the assailant's description. Penny knew the sheriff was a good man, a man of character and high ideals. His can-do attitude combined with his physical appearance – he was a few inches over six feet tall with strong angular facial features – left Penny convinced that her assailant would soon be apprehended.

She did her best to describe the man: 5'6" or 5'7", stocky build, brown eyes, long sandy hair with a scraggly beard. She said he was wearing long pants and had a black leather jacket on with buttons or snaps down the front. She thought he was about thirty.

Steven Avery came to Deputy Dvorak's mind immediately. Steve had long hair and a beard that would pass as scraggly in some circles, but he's nowhere near 5'6" or 5'7" – he's lucky if he's five feet tall. And his eyes aren't brown, they're blue. But it didn't matter to Deputy Dvorak – she knew it was Steven Avery, it just had to be.

Dvorak lived right across the street from Steve and Lori out on Old Highway Y, and she was familiar with some of his antics. She despised him, and she considered him just the sort of lowlife creep that would commit such a heinous crime. A few years earlier, she even saw him tether his two-year-old toddler to a tree to keep the child from wandering off. *So that's his idea of babysitting,* Dvorak thought at the time. *What a piece of work.*

She also knew Steve from his frequent stints in the county jail where she'd worked as a corrections officer before moving over to the patrol division. When she was asked at a deposition years later why she suspected Steven Avery so soon, Dvorak responded that he had "a look in his eyes" that made her feel uncomfortable. He was "a dirty man," she continued, and the first thing they did whenever he was placed in the slammer was get him in the shower – "the stench was that bad."

It's no wonder Steven Avery creeped out Dvorak. He had a record that dated back to when he was a juvenile, and some of his crimes were truly despicable. In September 1982, for instance, he and a friend had set a cat on fire. And just the previous year a neighbor's dog had returned home half-castrated, and the neighbor suspected Steve was behind that one too. He once threatened to run his former girlfriend off the road and shoot out her car windows. He told her he was going to put sugar in her gas tank, and a week later she found sand in her engine oil. He was so distraught over their break-up that he told her he was going to burn down his parents' house while they were inside.

But it was the crime Steve was out on bail for – the episode where he rammed into Sandy Murphy's car and then held her at gunpoint – that was most on Dvorak and Kocourek's minds. You don't victimize the wife of a deputy sheriff and expect it to go unnoticed, because the men and women in blue, or brown in the case of the Sheriff's Department, pay close attention when one of their own is the victim of a crime. It's human nature, and it's completely understandable.

And it's not just when they're victims. Cops don't miss it when a family member of one of their colleagues is on the wrong side of the law either, which is another reason why Steve might have come so quickly to Deputy Dvorak's mind. Steve's uncle Arland was a deputy at the Sheriff's Department, and it wasn't lost on Arland's fellow officers that his nephew

Steve was firmly planted on the wrong side of the law. So it wasn't surprising that within hours after Penny was attacked, there was "talk among the officers," as Dvorak later put it, that Steven Avery might have been the assailant.

After he and Dvorak settled on Avery as the likely assailant, Sheriff Kocourek promptly called the jail. He wanted a mug shot of Steve brought up to the hospital along with a dozen or so photos of other white males in their early thirties sporting beards. The deputy who answered the Sheriff's call could tell he meant business, and the photos arrived within minutes.

Kocourek stuffed the mug shots into his pocket and then summoned his Chief Deputy, Gene Kusche. Kusche was the nearest thing the department had to a police artist, and the Sheriff wanted him to work up a composite sketch of the suspect. Penny had been moved to a room on the second floor, and after pulling up a chair next to her bed, Kusche introduced himself and did his best to put Penny at ease – something that came natural to the affable, handle-bar mustached chief deputy.

Police sketches are basically head shots – they show what a suspect looks like from the neck up – and while facial hair limits the pool of potential suspects, it presents its own set of problems. The most obvious is that the suspect can alter his appearance by simply shaving off his beard. But there's another problem that's not as apparent. A bearded suspect's face is partially concealed, and to the extent that a victim is uncertain about a suspect's facial features, the reliability of the police sketch is diminished.

Penny's assailant was bearded, but she did her best to describe him anyhow, and Kusche worked on the sketch until, as he put it at trial, "the victim was satisfied in her mind that it was a reasonable representation of what her memory was." If his testimony sounds convoluted, perhaps there's a reason.

Kusche took great pride in his composite sketch of Penny's assailant. For one thing, it was his first. But mostly, it was so darn good. In fact, it was so good that over the years, more than a few who have seen it have commented that it looks *exactly* like Avery's mug shot. Even the trial judge referred to the two depictions as bearing an "uncanny resemblance" to each other.

With Kusche's composite sketch out of the way, it was time for Sheriff Kocourek to conduct the photo array. To hold up in Court, a photo array can't be "unduly suggestive." In other words, the police must show the victim photos of people who look like the suspect – the closer the better. So if the victim describes a bald man with a bulbous nose and three missing front teeth, for example, it won't do to show her one photo of the suspect and eight others of Matt Damon look-alikes.

The Sheriff brought out the stack of mug shots that he'd stuffed into his pocket a few hours earlier and assembled the photo array. With Kusche still in the room, he spread out nine photos on a table in front of Penny and asked her if she recognized the man who assaulted her. Penny picked out Avery immediately. She looked over the others just to make sure, and then she told the Sheriff that was the man who assaulted her. It was that simple. The Sheriff had what he needed, and he directed his night shift commander to take "the subject" into custody.

FOUR

IT WAS AFTER TEN that night when Steve and Lori
finally got home from Green Bay. The kids had fallen
asleep in the car and Lori got them down right after Steve
carried them in. They'd been on the go since nine that morning
and they were both exhausted, so they crawled into bed a little
after eleven.

Having given birth to the twins only six days earlier,
Lori was especially tired, but she couldn't fall asleep. Steve's
impulsive act of confronting Sandy Murphy on the road last
January weighed heavily on her mind and robbed her of the
peaceful night's sleep that sometimes comes from exhaustion.
Despite everything, she still loved Steve and she and the kids
needed him dearly. He was far from perfect, but he'd been
trying hard to improve since the incident with Sandy Murphy.
He was finally getting on track, not a perfect track, but a track
Lori could live with. Neither of them had unreasonable
expectations – financially or otherwise. Steve had his truck,
and Lori felt welcomed into his close-knit family. If only he

would have gotten control of himself last January and not pulled that stunt with Sandy Murphy.

Lori had asked him more than once what he was thinking. Sandy Murphy's identification of him was irrefutable, she was practically his neighbor! He did the crime, and now he'd do the time. In a few months, some judge would send him off to prison – the only question was for how long – and she'd be left to raise five young children all on her own. But what Lori didn't know was that a worse nightmare loomed right around the corner, a nightmare that would begin in less than an hour and one that would haunt her for the rest of her life.

* * *

Police exercise extreme caution when they take a bad guy into custody – especially when the man they're after is as dangerous as whoever it was that attacked Penny Beerntsen. Violent offenders are desperate to avoid apprehension since being caught usually lands them in prison, and while cops are committed to making the streets safe for the rest of us, they'd just as soon come home at night alive.

But self-preservation isn't the only thing police must consider when they make an arrest. From petty crimes like disturbing the peace, to more serious ones like sexual assault or murder, the Fourth Amendment's prohibition against unreasonable searches and seizures is the most litigated issue in trial and appellate courts all over the land. If police violate a suspect's constitutional rights, then the evidence that is derived, or as the law metaphorically puts it, "the fruits of the poisonous tree," will be suppressed, and the whole case might fail. And police must tread especially cautiously when it comes to our homes for "a man's home is his castle," so says the law. The rule is uncharacteristically clear: absent exigent circumstances or a warrant, the cops can't arrest a person in his or her home.

But Sheriff Kocourek must have missed that section of law enforcement training, for as soon as Penny Beerntsen identified Steven Avery as her assailant, he rounded up his men and sent them out to Steve and Lori's house to bring him in. In fact, the officers assigned to make the arrest even considered calling in the SWAT team. But fortunately, the night shift commander, Sergeant Ken Petersen, had a better idea. Maybe Arland Avery, Steve's uncle and a deputy on the Force, could get them in. They could make the arrest without incident that way, and everybody could go home alive. So Petersen called Arland, who was off duty but quickly agreed. Arland knew Lori and the kids were home sleeping, and the last thing he wanted was for the SWAT team to storm the house with guns a blazing.

So Sergeant Petersen along with Deputies Jim Froelich and Mike Bushman gathered at Arland's house at eleven thirty. The four of them huddled together and formulated a plan. Arland and Froelich would enter from the rear while Petersen covered the front while Bushman and his canine unit "Duke" would float the perimeter in case Steve tried to escape.

Arland knocked on the door just before midnight, but nobody answered so he gave a "slight push," and the door magically opened.

"Lori," he shouted, as he and Deputy Froelich walked in, "where are you?"

Lori heard the dog barking in the back yard a few minutes earlier and wondered if someone was out there. "Upstairs," she shouted back.

"Where's Steve? I need to talk to him," Arland yelled from the landing half way up the stairs.

Steve woke up to the shouting and walked warily down the stairs. Froelich had ducked into a closet underneath the stairwell, and as Steve walked past he sneaked behind him and followed him into the kitchen where Sergeant Petersen was waiting. Froelich told Steve to turn around, and then he handcuffed him. According to Froelich's report, Petersen advised Steve he was under arrest for "suspicion of attempted murder" – without mentioning anything about a sexual assault.

Still upstairs, Lori fell onto the bed when she heard someone tell Steve he was under arrest, but she quickly got herself together and went downstairs to find out what was going on. When she walked into her kitchen, she saw two police officers standing next to Steve. He had handcuffs on, and someone with a flashlight was reading him his rights.

"Would someone please tell me what's going on?" Lori asked.

Sergeant Petersen told her he was sorry, but he couldn't say anything.

Directing her question to her husband this time, Lori asked again, "What's going on?"

According to Froelich and Petersen, Steve looked at his wife and said, "They said I tried to murder some girl." The significance of Steve's response was hotly disputed at trial. The prosecution seized on the comment. The officers hadn't said anything to suggest that the victim was female, the prosecutor argued, so since Mr. Avery knew the victim was a woman, he must have committed the crime. Steve's lawyer, on the other hand, considered the argument pretty thin.

Sergeant Petersen possessed a quality that would serve him well years later when he succeeded Tom Kocourek as the Sheriff – he doesn't beat around the bush. So he asked Steve point blank in the squad that night, "Did you assault Penny Beerntsen?" and Steve replied with an equally direct "no." Then Petersen asked him if he was on the beach, and Steve denied that too – he said he was pouring concrete at his dad's salvage yard, and then he and his family went up to Green Bay.

27

The Sheriff was waiting for Steve when he arrived at the jail – he planned to ask him a few questions of his own. But Steve stuck to his guns, or as Kocourek put it in his report, "he denied any involvement in the incident, admitting to nothing." He hadn't worked a case in years, but the Sheriff still had some of the detective in him, and he wanted to make sure the follow-up investigation was done right. He was certain Steve was lying and that his family would lie for him too. So before leaving the jail that night, he instructed the jail staff not to permit any phone calls or visits with Steve. As he put it in his report, "Steve is using his family as an alibi for his whereabouts, and I wish to question them without affording Steve the opportunity of establishing a phony alibi."

* * *

Lori Avery didn't sleep after Steve was arrested that night. There must be some mistake, she thought, he was with her all day. She called Steve's mom and dad at six in the morning and told them how the police barged in at midnight and arrested their son.

Allan Avery tried calling the jail, but the dayshift commander told him the Sheriff had denied all phone calls and visits with his son until further notice. Undeterred, Mr. Avery called Captain Don Belz. It was seven in the morning, but Allan knew Belz, and he called him at home.

"What's going on with my son," Mr. Avery demanded, "he was working with me all day, pouring cement. They don't have no right taking him out of his house like that – after all, a guy's got some rights."

Captain Belz told Mr. Avery he didn't know anything about it – he works days, not nights – but he'd check it out and get right back to him. But Belz never got back to Allan Avery.

Years later, he told a private investigator the Sheriff told him if he did, he'd be fired.

Sheriff Kocourek called the DA first thing in the morning and told him he needed a search warrant. He wanted to search Steven Avery's residence for physical evidence – blood, hair, semen, that sort of thing – and anything else that might be evidence of the crime. He told the DA he was convinced that Avery was the assailant, and he was determined to bring him to justice. The DA made the arrangements with the Judge, and by ten thirty, the Sheriff and his deputies were knocking at Lori's door with a search warrant in hand.

The Sheriff had a few questions for Lori while the deputies executed the warrant. He wanted to know her husband's whereabouts in the late afternoon hours on the day before. Lori told him Steve couldn't have done whatever they were accusing him of – he was with her all day. They were at his parents' salvage yard for most of the afternoon, and Steve was outside pouring concrete with the guys while she was visiting with her in-laws inside. Lori explained that Steve came in just as *Divorce Court* ended at three-thirty and told her to get the kids ready. Then, as Kocourek qualified it in his report, she and Steve "reportedly" drove to Green Bay.

Not a bad alibi, Kocourek thought to himself, *but it doesn't prove a thing. She was in the house the whole time while Steve was supposedly outside pouring concrete – he was out of her sight for hours. She doesn't know what he was up to. Besides, she's probably lying.*

But Lori wasn't the only one to tell police that Steven Avery couldn't have committed the assault. His parents and almost a dozen family members and friends of the family gave the same account that Steve and Lori did, and even though they hadn't spoken with Steve or with each other, their stories all matched.

As for the search warrant, the Sheriff and his men found little that interested them. But they took it anyhow. A pair of cut-off shorts, a brown tee shirt, some black socks, black dress shoes, some more tee shirts, and two pairs of blue jeans. They also took the floor mat from the driver's side of Steve's 1976 Chevy Blazer, hoping the crime lab would find some embedded grains of Lake Michigan sand.

Kocourek knew they'd have to establish a time-frame to show that Avery had time to commit the assault, and he knew it would be close. Penny Beerntsen had been an excellent reporter of time. It was ten to four when the man first grabbed her, and he scampered into the woods fifteen minutes later at five minutes after four. If Avery really was at the Shopko in Green Bay like his wife says he was, he better find out precisely what time they were there.

So the next day, the Sheriff sent out his men to do some more digging. Detective Fred Nicholson drove up to Green Bay and spoke with the check-out clerk at ShopKo. Sure, she remembered the family with the newborn twins – she couldn't believe they'd bring infants to such a public place, with so many germs and everything. The manager retrieved the data: the paint was purchased at 5:11 that afternoon.

That left between 4:05 and 5:11 – only sixty-six minutes to run the half mile to the parking lot – in street clothes no less, rush to the Salvage Yard to pick up Lori and the kids, and be in the checkout lane at ShopKo thirty miles north in Green Bay. *Sixty-six minutes to do all that*, Detective Nicholson thought, *there wouldn't be any wiggle room.*

So he drove to the crime-scene and made a dry run. Intermittently running and walking at a fast pace, it took him thirteen minutes to get from where Duke the police dog found Penny's bathing suit to the parking lot, and another forty-four minutes to drive up to ShopKo in Green Bay, grab a gallon of paint, and walk to the checkout lane. Fifty-seven minutes in all, and the Sheriff had his time-frame – with nine minutes to spare! Never mind that Nicholson later testified he "averaged 10 miles an hour over the limit, but never more than 15 over." Or that he didn't account for the time it would take to load five children into a truck, including two infants, stop at a fast-food restaurant and then a car wash, and check the paint section at ShopKo for a leftover can of paint on sale. No matter, they had their man. It was Steven Avery – it just had to be!

FIVE

DRESSED IN BRIGHT orange jail garb, Steven Avery was brought before the Court Commissioner the next day for a bail hearing. District Attorney Denis Vogel informed the Court he was charging the defendant with first degree sexual assault and attempted murder. Vogel requested $50,000 cash bail, and the Court Commissioner agreed – Steve wasn't going anywhere this time.

Denis Vogel had been the district attorney for just over eight years when Penny Beerntsen was attacked on the beach that day. A Manitowoc native, he was from a prominent farm family that stretched back more than a hundred years. With his close cropped mustache, plastered on hair, and three piece suits, he looked every bit the part of a young aggressive attorney, and he made up for his small stature and squeaky voice with a quick tongue and sharp wit.

Nobody's ever known an Avery that could post $50,000 cash bail, but Vogel wasn't about to take any chances. The state legislature had recently added to the prosecution's arsenal a new crime-fighting weapon called a "Petition for Pretrial Preventive Detention." The new law permitted the Court to detain an accused awaiting trial without bail if release on bail would not "adequately protect members of the community from serious bodily harm." The statute only applied to a handful of specifically enumerated felonies and first degree sexual assault and attempted murder weren't on the list, so Vogel knew he'd be pushing the envelope if he filed one in this case.

He called a friend at the Attorney General's Office who cautioned him that the law probably didn't apply. But it didn't matter to the aggressive young prosecutor. Vogel apparently recorded his telephone calls and had his conversations transcribed, so there's a record of the call. Here's a portion:

"Hi Mike – Denis Vogel calling."

"Denis, how are you? I'm sorry not to get to you sooner but I've been tied up in a telephone call, a couple of phone calls since 7:30."

"You work harder than I do, Mike."

"I was here at quarter to seven so don't give me that shit, I beat you in."

"Jesus Christ. Say, listen, I got a pre-trial detention hearing tomorrow."

"Okay."

"On a fellow that was charged with attempted first degree murder and second degree sexual assault, and I'm wondering what type of evidence you recommend putting in to show dangerousness to the community or whatever it is – hang on, let me get my statute book.

"She's a real respectable lady in town," Vogel continued, "and her husband has a very good business. Basically, she's a very – she comes from a good family, she just happened to be jogging down the beach, gets grabbed, you know, he goes after her and tries to rape her."

"He's tried to establish somewhat of an alibi by claiming he wasn't there. His family members are going to support him, but I think when it comes down to it, it's going to be her word saying it's positively him vs. him saying he didn't do it. But I've got him. He's been convicted of burglary before and he's out on bail right now on two counts of endangering safety by conduct regardless of life."

"You see my problem is this," Vogel continued, "The guy doesn't have a prior conviction for a violent crime, as required under paragraph one. But you know – what's the worst thing that could happen?"

The Assistant AG tried to reel Vogel in: "I think you've got trouble with that attempt charge, Denis, I really do. I remember at the time they passed this thing they tried to make it as tight as possible because, you know, trying to get something like this through this legislature, which is very liberal by and large – at least the committee chairman and the chairpersons in the right committees are very liberal – and I think everything was tightened up as much as possible. I think that was the intent when I looked at this thing."

But Vogel would have none of it: "Alright, listen Mike, thanks a lot, I appreciate it. I got it scheduled for tomorrow. Who knows, it might be a good case to appeal."

As a practical matter, Vogel's petition meant nothing. Steve and Lori didn't have a pot to pee in, and Steve's parents didn't have that kind of money lying around either. But it didn't matter – Vogel smelled blood in the water. He filed his petition and the Judge granted it the following day. It was official – Steven Avery was "preventively detained".

* * *

To Lori, of course, it didn't matter whether Steve was being detained under some stupid new law or held on high cash bail – either way, he wasn't coming home. She was left alone to care for five young children who were starting to wonder where their dad was, and all she could do was hope and pray.

Steven Avery with his family the day before his arrest

But hoping and praying didn't seem to be working after awhile, so Lori did what many inmates' loved ones do when they don't know where else to turn – she wrote a letter to the Judge:

> Dear Judge Hazelwood,
>   I am writing this on behalf of Steven Avery. Steve along with myself, Lori (his wife), and his family and friends do not understand why he cannot be put up on bail. How can the law hold an innocent

man when we have witnesses as to his whereabouts and the State only has her word.

I was brought up to believe in the laws and that people have rights, and since my husband has been arrested, I no longer believe in either one. I thought people along with law enforcement officers did not have the right to walk into someone else's home, in this case late at night, without permission and arrest someone without a warrant for that person's arrest.

I am left out here by myself to raise five children who all miss their daddy very much. I don't really believe that there are too many people in the world who could take as much stuff as I have since July 19th. In a brief summary, I have gone from false labor to real labor to emergency surgery (c-section) to getting out with restrictions of no heavy or exerting work to having my husband arrested for something he didn't do to being left alone with our five kids – and no one seems to care.

I am now talking (by phone) to Steve and he would like to say a few words: Judge, I am innocent and I'm not lying, I'll take a lie detector test to prove it. I like you a lot but I don't understand how they can hold me on such little evidence. … Is there any way the motions can be heard by the end of the month and any chance of me getting out on the motions. Could you please help me and my family? I would really appreciate it. Thank you Judge. Steve

I am sorry for taking out so much of your time. Thank you for listening.

Sincerely, Lori Avery

P.S. Could you please let me or Steve know what you think.

What can a judge do when he or she receives a letter like that – when a woman painfully pleads for justice on behalf of her husband and her children, but doesn't know where to turn? Unfortunately, not much, for the law refers to judges as "neutral and detached magistrates," and as such, they aren't supposed to side with one party or the other. So all Judge Hazlewood could do was forward copies of Lori's letter to the district attorney and defense counsel and hope they'd respond.

SIX

WOUNDS SLOWLY HEALING, Penny Beerntsen was at home two days after the assault when the telephone rang:

"Hello ... hello," Penny answered.

"What are you doing?" asked the caller.

"Who do you want?"

"I want you."

Penny hung up the phone. "Oh my God, he knows who I am, he has our telephone number and he probably knows where we live!" She called Tom and he told her to call the Sheriff. He'd be right home.

Sheriff Kocourek stepped up security immediately. He had Dispatch send out a teletype to all squads – until further notice the Sheriff wanted a squad at the Beerntsens' residence around the clock. He also put a tracer on the phone in case the suspect called again.

Who called Penny Beerntsen two days after she was attacked? It wasn't Steven Avery – he was in jail under the

38

Sheriff's order prohibiting him from making any telephone calls. But if the Sheriff and the DA considered the question, there isn't any evidence in the record suggesting it. Which begs the question – why not?

Even though she wasn't a detective, Kocourek assigned Deputy Dvorak to do some of the follow-up investigation on the Avery case. Penny would have to recount the embarrassing details of the assault to complete strangers as the case wound its way through the justice system, and the Sheriff thought the least he could do was limit the number of officers she'd have to confide in. Besides, as a woman, Deputy Dvorak understood what Penny went through – at least more than a male detective could, and she was emotionally involved in the case from the start. She even brought some cut flowers from her garden to Penny before she was released from the hospital the morning after the assault.

The Sheriff sent Dvorak out to Penny's home to re-interview her a few days after the assault. Something wasn't adding up. When they asked Penny at the hospital if the assailant's hands were greasy, Penny's answer was clear – no, his hands weren't greasy, they were clean. But Steven Avery's hands were perpetually greasy because he worked on cars so much. Even the clerk at ShopKo noticed his hands were greasy when he was in the check-out lane just an hour after Penny was assaulted. So Deputy Dvorak asked Penny again, "Did the assailant have anything on his hands, anything – grease, oil, cement?" But Penny was no less certain this time – "no," she said, "his hands were clean."

After the interview, Dvorak and Penny drove downtown to the Big Boy restaurant where they killed some time before walking over to the Sheriff's Department. The Sheriff had set up a line-up to see if Penny could identify her assailant again. Deputy Dvorak escorted Penny into a dark

39

hallway with a one way glass window that looked into a larger room on the other side. Tom Beerntsen was already there, so was Kocourek and Vogel, and an assistant public defender was also there to observe the circumstances of the line-up. Penny slowly viewed the eight men in the line-up, and although it took a long time, she eventually placed a checkmark after number six on form. Success – she'd picked out Avery again!

The defense later challenged the line-up in Court. Asked how long the victim viewed the participants, the assistant public defender testified, "I'd estimate between eight and ten minutes, probably closer to ten." She claimed one of the participants looked at Avery during most of the line-up, and in her opinion, Steven Avery stuck out like a sore thumb: "He was the youngest, the fairest, possibly the shortest – he left a distinct impression." She also testified that she had to ask Tom Beerntsen not to talk to his wife during the line-up procedure and that she wasn't able to see the form after Penny marked it because she immediately gave it to the Sheriff and walked out of the room.

The line-up – Steven Avery is #6

With another identification of the assailant under his belt, Sheriff Kocourek felt confident about the case, and with

40

his wife's assailant locked securely behind bars, Tom Beerntsen wanted to thank the police officers and the EMTs who came to Penny's aid. So the Sheriff sent him their names, and while he was at it, he included some prudent advice for his friend:

> Tom, I realize that you are intending to thank these people individually. I wish to point out that a simple letter acknowledging their professionalism and dedication, to be placed in their personnel file, goes a long way."

> Tom Kocourek

SEVEN

EVERY DAY, PROSECUTORS, defense attorneys, and judges in county courthouses across the land do the heavy lifting on the front lines of the criminal justice system. Thousands of cases flow through, each with its own set of facts – a few complicated, but most of them not. Prosecutors start the ball rolling by summoning offenders into Court with criminal complaints, and the ball doesn't stop rolling until the case is resolved. They carry boxes loaded with files to "Intake Court," where scores of lawyers and unrepresented defendants wait patiently for the judge to call their case so they can take their turn at the table and enter their plea – "Not guilty, Your Honor." There are initial appearances, preliminary examinations, arraignments, settlement conferences, motion hearings, plea hearings, pretrial conferences, and the occasional trial.

In the Avery case, assistant public defender Reesa Evans-Marcinczyk was appointed to represent the accused. She would come to believe so firmly in Steve's innocence that she refused to go to the beach to observe where Penny was attacked for fear the assailant might still be out there. She filed eighteen motions in the days immediately following Avery's arrest. There was a motion for everything – to suppress, to exclude, to compel, and, of course, to dismiss. You name it, she moved for it.

But Evans-Marcinczyk became ill a few months into the case, and another attorney was appointed to replace her. Although no longer a participant in the legal proceedings, as the years went by, Evans-Marcinczyk never wavered in her belief that Avery was innocent.

Attorney Jim Bolgert of Sheboygan was appointed successor counsel. Bolgert, who went on to serve as a circuit court judge in Sheboygan County, one county south of Manitowoc, promptly requested an adjournment of the Motion Hearing to allow him time to prepare.

Judge Fred Hazlewood was on Intake when the charges were filed. Affectionately known as Judge Fred, Judge Hazlewood liked to keep cases moving along swiftly, but he also knew that Jim Bolgert would need time to prepare for the boatload of motions filed by Evans-Marcinczyk, so he granted a three week adjournment and set aside a full day for the hearing.

On the day of the hearing, the Judge and the parties methodically addressed the motions, one at a time. Number one on the docket was the defendant's Motion to Change Venue. Jim Bolgert argued that extensive media coverage of the assault had made it impossible for his client to receive a fair trial in Manitowoc County. The local radio and TV stations had covered the case extensively – even the *Milwaukee Journal* ran a story about the assault on the shore of Lake Michigan up in Manitowoc County.

But concluding that the publicity wasn't so "widespread or salacious or prejudicial" that it would deny the defendant a fair trial, Judge Hazlewood denied the defendant's request to change venue. The trial would be held in Manitowoc County.

Not surprisingly, though, the parties spent most of their time at the Motion Hearing on the defendant's request to suppress Penny's identification of Avery as her assailant. Jim Bolgert called Judy Dvorak, Gene Kusche, and the Sheriff himself to the stand and painstakingly questioned each of them about the procedures they used to obtain his client's I.D.

But Judge Hazlewood didn't buy it. In his November 13, 1985 "Memorandum to Supplement Oral Decision," he ruled that "the preparation of a composite drawing prior to showing the complaining witness a photo lineup was particularly appropriate in this case. And as noted, both the Sheriff and the deputy who initially interviewed Ms. Beerntsen considered the possibility that the defendant was involved in this assault."

In a sentence brimming with irony given how things turned out, the Judge continued: "This additional check, arguably unnecessary, provides an added assurance that Deputy Dvorak and Sheriff Kocourek's initial suspicions did not become a self-fulfilling prophecy when Ms. Beerntsen selected the defendant's photograph." Motion denied.

Jim Bolgert fought valiantly, but most of the motions filed by Evans-Marcinczyk were perfunctory, and the Court granted only two of them: the Motion to Suppress Avery's statement to Sheriff Kocourek – which didn't hurt the State anyhow since Avery told the Sheriff he was innocent – the Motion for Access to the Crime Lab Analyst.

* * *

After three or four years in the business, prosecutors and defense attorneys know what a case is worth. They know whether the State has the goods for a conviction or if there's a realistic defense. They know the parameters of what the Judge is likely to do at sentencing, and they know when each other are bluffing. As a result, most criminal cases are resolved by plea bargains, which aren't as tawdry as the press makes them sound. Like making sausage, the process is ugly, but the end product is usually palatable as long as everyone does their job.

Then there are trials, which are animals of a completely different stripe. Amidst the chaos, most lawyers can tell early on which files are likely to go to trial. They're usually close cases where the charges are serious and the stakes are high. And most lawyers know the feeling – that slight discomfort that begins about six weeks before the trial. It's been months since the charges were filed and the early skirmishes in court have faded from memory, and for the press of other matters, they've neglected the file. Then, depending on the complexity of the case and how much stomach discomfort the lawyer can handle, the increasingly nervous attorney performs a cursory review to spot problems that will be fatal if they're not addressed immediately. Eventually they carve out several hours from their calendar and review the entire file, flagging the most important portions, while continually shrinking the information into a more manageable size. But despite their best intentions to have every detail nailed down early enough to get a good night's sleep on the night before trial, most of them are invariably still up working well into the night.

A few weeks before trial, Bolgert and Vogel sparred over whether the defense should have access to records relating to counseling services that Penny received in the weeks immediately after the assault. Penny diffused the controversy herself by consenting to their release, but in this letter to the Court, she relayed her concerns:

Dear Judge Hazelwood:

45

I didn't want Mr. Vogel to turn over my counseling records without this accompanying comment on the impact of my decision to cooperate in this matter. I'm not sure Mr. Bolgert fully comprehends the import of his request, though I am sure it was made in good faith and in the spirit of providing Mr. Steven Avery with the best possible defense.

Discussions which occur between therapist and client are privileged information, as I'm sure all parties involved in this case are aware. When a person decides to enter into counseling he/she is aware of the confidentiality of all conversations that occur in the privacy of the therapist's office. It is one of the basic tenets of psychotherapy and essential to the establishment of a trusting relationship between client and therapist. Without this fundamental principle there can be no meaningful therapeutic progress.

Additionally, I am concerned that I may be setting a dangerous precedent for future victims of violent crime. I do not want any other victim to delay or rule out therapy due to fear that what is said in the privacy of a psychologist's office may become part of the public record.

But I have made peace with the fact that it is essential to turn these records over to the Court; I do not object if you turn them over in their entirety to Mr. Bolgert. I have nothing to hide and want to cooperate fully in order that justice might best be served.

Thank you for your careful consideration of this issue.

Sincerely yours,
Penny Beerntsen

It's not unusual for a last minute surprise to surface just days before trial, and in his December 6 letter to Jim Bolgert, Denis Vogel had one for the defense:

> Dear Jim,
>
> In speaking with three witnesses, Deputy Froelich, Judy Dvorak, and Ken Petersen, all three officers have had prior contact with Steve Avery, the defendant, and will be in a position to testify that they have personally seen Mr. Avery wearing a leather motorcycle type jacket, dark brownish in color, which would be short waist length.

It was more bad news for the defense.

They say a criminal defense attorney's worst nightmare is to defend someone who's innocent – what if you lose? Most people charged with a serious crime are guilty. They better be or the prosecutor has no business charging them. But once in a great while, a defense lawyer comes across a client who they're almost certain is innocent. And so it was for Jim Bolgert. He knew the State's case was weak – it relied almost entirely on the victim's identification of the defendant, and eyewitness identifications are notoriously unreliable. If he could effectively attack the ID and present a strong alibi defense, his client stood half a chance.

But while trials aim for objective truth, the influence of emotion is never completely divorced from human affairs, and Bolgert knew that the State would own the emotional subtext in this one. With the Avery clan and their salvage yard sheep sheds on one side, and Penny and Tom Beerntsen and their storied candy store on the other, the intangibles were not on his side.

EIGHT

SCHEDULED TO BEGIN on December 9, 1985, just two weeks before Christmas, the Defense couldn't have drawn a worse time for the trial. For an acquittal, the jury would have to pay the closest attention, and the defense would have to be nearly unassailable. But with sugarplums and last minute shopping dancing in their heads, the jurors would likely be distracted, and the last thing they'd want to do is re-victimize Penny Beerntsen by acquitting her assailant right before Christmas.

The first day of the trial finally arrived. In order to accommodate the large number of people in the jury pool, Judge Hazlewood conducted jury selection in Branch 1, the most spacious of the three courtrooms. The lawyers scurried about down to the last minute, or maybe a few beyond, and if they were like most trial attorneys, they'd probably downed three or four cups of coffee and made their final stop at the restroom just in time.

The clerk assembled the panel of prospective jurors, and Judge Hazlewood addressed them for the first time: "Ladies and gentlemen, the case we're going to be trying today is the *State of Wisconsin vs. Steven A. Avery*. Appearing and representing the State is District Attorney Denis Vogel."

The prosecutor stood and greeted the jurors, "Good morning everybody."

"Sitting next to Mr. Vogel is Sheriff Tom Kocourek for Manitowoc County."

"Good morning."

"Representing the defendant is Attorney James Bolgert – Mr. Bolgert?"

"Good morning."

"And seated next to Mr. Bolgert is the defendant, Steven Avery – Mr. Avery?"

"Good morning," the Defendant managed a soft reply.

"Are counsel ready for trial?"

"Yes, Your Honor," Vogel and Bolgert answered in unison.

Warning the jurors not to consider the charges, themselves, as evidence against the defendant, Judge Hazlewood read them out loud:

> Count 1: On or about the 29th of July, 1985, in the Township of Two Rivers, in said County and State, the defendant did unlawfully have sexual contact with another person without the consent of that person and by the threat of use of a dangerous weapon, to wit: by the threat of the use of a knife, contrary to 940.225(1)(d) of the Wisconsin Statutes.

The jury gulped, and Judge Fred continued:

Count 2: At the same time and place, the defendant did unlawfully attempt to cause the death of another human being with intent to kill that person, contrary to Sections 940.01 and 939.32(1)(a) of the Wisconsin Statutes.

They gulped again, and the Judge read the final charge – false imprisonment:

Count 3: At the same time and place, the defendant did unlawfully and intentionally restrain another without that person's consent and with knowledge that he had no lawful authority to do so; contrary to Section 940.30 of the Wisconsin Statutes.

If you've ever sat on a jury in a criminal case, then you've heard a version of Judge Hazlewood's final instruction, and if you were Steven Avery that day, you hoped like hell they were paying attention:

To the charges I have just read, the defendant has entered a plea of not guilty, which means a denial of every material allegation in the Information. The law presumes every person charged with the commission of an offense to be innocent, this presumption attends the defendant; that is, it stays with the defendant, throughout the trial and prevails at its close unless it is overcome by evidence which satisfies a jury of guilt beyond a reasonable doubt. The defendant is not required to prove his innocence. The burden of proving the defendant guilty of every element of the crime charged is upon the State. Before you can return a verdict of guilty, the State must prove to your satisfaction beyond a reasonable doubt that the defendant is guilty.

Thankfully, all but the most jaded jurors actually take that instruction seriously. They might be incensed by the charges, and maybe even put off by the appearance of the defendant, but they also know that his life, or at least a good part of it, is in their hands.

* * *

With Manitowoc County's population at just over eighty thousand, there's a good chance that some of the jurors know one of the parties, one of the attorneys, or maybe a witness or two, and the Avery trial was no exception. Several jurors knew of Steve's family's unsavory reputation, and for those who didn't, they'd soon find out since the entire jury pool was present for everyone's answers.

With Bolgert and Vogel holding their breaths, Judge Hazlewood popped the Court's first question: "Are there any among you who are acquainted with or know either the defendant, Steven Avery, or a member of his immediate family?"

Several jurors raised their hands, and starting with Juror No. 8, Judge Hazlewood explored their potential for bias:

"Ms. R *(the author has excluded the jurors' names)*, how long have you known either the defendant or his family?"

"About seventeen years."

"And do you have regular contact with the family?"

"No."

"Or the defendant?"

"Not any longer."

"When was the last time you saw either the defendant or a family member?"

"It would have been quite a while ago, I'm a schoolteacher."

"That's how you happen to know the family?"

"Yes."

"Because of your relationship with the family – we won't probe into that in any detail – do you feel that you would tend to give greater or lesser weight to one side over the other?"

"I would try not to."

"Do you feel it would be difficult for you to judge the case fairly and impartially, strictly on the evidence that is produced at the trial and excluding everything else?"

"I would try not to."

"So do you think it would be possible for you to judge this case fairly and impartially after you have heard the evidence, without bringing any preconceived notions one way or the other into your deliberations?"

"I would hope that would be the case, yes."

"Do you think there's a possibility that you would not be able to do so?"

"I guess I would have some question."

Judge Hazlewood did exactly what he should have under the law – he excused Ms. R for cause.

Juror No. 10, who'd also raised her hand, was an even easier call:

"Ms. S, do you know the defendant or his family?"

"Yes, I do."

"How long have you known them?"

"Six years."

"Six years?"

"Yup."

"Do you feel it would be difficult for you to judge this case fairly and impartially because of your prior knowledge of the defendant or his family?"

"Yes."

Judge Hazlewood ended the colloquy: "The Court will excuse Juror No. 10."

Then Juror No. 26 piped in out of the blue: "It doesn't have anything to do with this, but I do know somebody who's a neighbor of the accused and I've heard that..."

Judge Hazlewood cut him off: "We don't want to know what you've heard. We'll get into that later."

Other prospective jurors knew Denis Vogel, and still others knew some of the police officers who would testify – more bad signs for the defense.

Again, Judge Hazlewood: "Are there any among you who is acquainted with or knows District Attorney Denis Vogel?"

Juror No. 2 raised his hand.

"Mr. H, how long have you known Mr. Vogel?"

"About five years."

"Is that a business or a personal relationship?"

"We're neighbors."

"You live right next door to Mr. Vogel?"

"Same block, three doors down."

"Do you feel that because you live on the same block, and Mr. Vogel will have to go home sometime and you'll see him, that there might be cause for you to give greater or lesser weight to one side in this case over the other?"

"None whatsoever, Your Honor."

Juror No. 2 stayed.

Juror No. 5 was a teacher, and Vogel had recently led a discussion for one of her high school classes. No. 5 said she could be fair – so she stayed.

Then there was Juror No. 15: "Mr. Vogel spoke at a tavern league meeting I was at."

"Do you think that would affect your judgment one way or the other?"

"No, it wouldn't, Your Honor."

53

Even more jurors knew the Sheriff. No. 27 served with him on an advisory panel for Wisconsin Public Service; No. 11 was the Maple Grove town constable; No. 22 knew him since 1979 when they were both realtors – "We spoke at church just last Sunday, Your Honor."

But each of them professed impartiality so they survived being struck for cause.

One of the jurors knew Chief Deputy Gene Kusche through the VFW: "He's the commander right now."

Another belonged to the same parish as Deputy Froelich – she went to grade school with his daughter.

Another knew Froelich's wife from working on church committees together, and still another was his neighbor.

Detective Conrad was the Cub Scout den leader for the son of Juror No. 10.

But each of them pledged fairness, so they stayed.

Denis Vogel knew he would face an onslaught of alibi witnesses when the defense presented its case, so when it was his turn to address the panel he tried to soften the blow:

"Members of the jury – if one side calls more witnesses than the other would you weigh that in favor of that side?

"As an example," Vogel continued, "If I were to call only one witness to the stand and the defense called fifteen witnesses, would you give the defense more weight than my one witness?"

And when it was Jim Bolgert's turn, he knew that with such an awful jury pool for the defense, he couldn't afford to beat around the bush: "Do any of you think just because Steve is sitting here, the chances are better than not that he's guilty? Anybody think that way?"

"As you already know, the charges are serious," Bolgert told them, "attempted murder, sexual assault – are any of those accusations so emotional for any of you that you won't be able to make your decision rationally? Do any of you think those accusations are so serious that you couldn't find anybody charged with them not guilty?"

Nobody raised their hands, but Jim Bolgert had his doubts. True, he could use his peremptory challenges to strike those who were unfavorably disposed toward his client, but each side only gets six strikes, and given the make-up of the panel, he could have used three times that many.

After lunch, Judge Hazlewood, the two attorneys, and the defendant retired to the Judge's chambers to conduct individual *voir dire* – which is a fancy way of saying that they questioned the prospective jurors in private. It's used to ferret out information from each juror, one at a time, about what they've heard about the case from the media or from other sources without poisoning the entire jury pool. It's a tiresome process, and it took all afternoon.

Finally, it was time to select the jury, and with everyone back in the courtroom, the lawyers alternated making their peremptory strikes until they'd each struck six. The panel of twenty six prospective jurors was winnowed down to fourteen – twelve would deliberate Steve's fate and two alternates would be randomly excused at the end of the trial.

The jury was sworn in at 5:25 p.m. and Judge Hazlewood gave the chosen ones their final instruction for the day: "I would ask everybody to talk about anything other than the case, what you may have heard or read about the case. How the Packers played in the fourth quarter last night is a perfectly legitimate discussion and anything else you can think of, but not the case. Relax, come back tomorrow morning refreshed, and we'll begin the trial."

Sitting on a jury is a sacrifice. It's the most important civic duty most of us will ever be called upon to fulfill. To do it right, we must give of ourselves – our time, our effort, and our sense of fairness. After all, somebody's liberty is at stake, and in some states someone's life is on the line.

Jury selection is also where a good judge can set the right tone and provide both sides with a fair trial, and that's exactly what Judge Hazlewood did in the Avery trial. He was not only fair and impartial, but with his kind and down-to-earth demeanor, he also made jury duty as painless as possible – and as always, he did it with a great sense of humor.

Anticipating widespread media attention that might improperly influence the outcome of the trial, he decided early on to sequester the jury. So the jurors stayed at the Budgetel across the street from the Courthouse, and in a memo to the bailiff outlining the procedure he wanted followed, the Judge even covered whether the jurors could imbibe: "This is Wisconsin, so the jurors may purchase up to two alcoholic beverages during the evening hours. However, no alcohol will be allowed during any period in which the panel is deliberating on a verdict."

There's no record as to how much the jury imbibed on the first night before trial, but we do know that they dined at the Colonial Inn. The "Inn" has since been restored, and it's now known as the Courthouse Pub, which is widely viewed among locals, tourists, and businessmen alike as one of East-Central Wisconsin's finest restaurants.

NINE

T HE TRIAL BEGAN in earnest the next morning. After breakfast at the Big Boy restaurant next door to the Budgetel, the jurors were escorted across the street and up the stairs of the Courthouse. Now that the actual trial was set to begin, the proceedings shifted over to Judge Hazlewood's regular courtroom. Its close quarters were well suited to Judge Fred's warm personality and his commitment to connect with the troubled young men and women who appeared in front of him over the years.

But there was nothing cozy or comforting about the Judge's courtroom on the first morning of trial. Nerves were frayed – especially those of the attorneys. They'd been living and breathing the case for weeks and they were anxious to get the show on the road. Judge Hazlewood, too, was determined to get things moving.

Trying a case is like telling a story – you must capture the jury's attention from the beginning and never let go until the case is in their hands. If you're unlucky enough to sit on a jury where a lawyer doesn't get it – if he starts with a minor drab witness, hides the main witnesses in the middle, and then muddles through to the end – it's a safe bet he's either fresh out of law school or he should probably be drafting wills and probating estates instead.

But Denis Vogel knew what he was doing, and he started strong. He led off with Penny Beerntsen, whose harrowing account of her assault captured the jury's attention immediately. First, he rapidly covered her biographical information – married, 36-years-old, a 12-year-old daughter and a 10-year-old son. And then he zeroed in on the afternoon of the assault.

Penny told the jury they arrived at Neshotah Park at 2:30 and staked out their claim in the sand, and with Vogel leading, she said it was precisely three o'clock when she said goodbye to Tom and the kids and started off on her run.

"So did you look at your watch?" Vogel asked.

"Yes, I did," Penny replied.

"And did you keep your watch on while you were running?"

"Yes."

Penny explained how she passed the strange looking man with the black leather jacket and jogged the rest of her route before turning around. Vogel had her slow down when she told them she saw the same man again on her way back laying in wait for her near a poplar tree. She explained how she tried to avoid him by jogging into the water, but he lunged at her and grabbed her from behind.

"What happened next?" Vogel asked.

"I twisted to try and get away. I yelled out to the sailboat, 'Help, help,' hoping someone would hear me. Then he tightened his grip around my neck and cut off my windpipe, so I was no longer able to scream."

Sparing none of the gruesome details, Vogel had Penny describe how the assailant manhandled her over the sand dunes and tried to rape her at the edge of the woods.

Penny was particularly effective when she described what happened when the man found out she wouldn't give in:

"What happened next?" Vogel asked.

"I was able to kick the man in the groin," Penny replied, "but then he put both hands around my neck and began strangling me."

"Did he say anything?"

Penny quoted her assailant: "'Now, I'm gonna kill you – you're gonna fucking die.'"

Vogel continued, "Then what happened?"

"He was shaking me up and down so hard that my head and upper back were hitting the ground. Both his hands were around my neck – my windpipe, and he was kneeling over me. He was grabbing me so tight I couldn't breathe. He kept saying, 'Now are you gonna do it? Are you gonna do it?' I remember thinking he was going to kill me if I didn't cooperate, but I couldn't say anything because I couldn't get any air."

Later, Vogel asked Penny how she felt after her assailant unexpectedly left.

"I was bruised, I was bloody, I was unable to move," she replied, "It felt like my arms and legs were made of lead. I was dazed. I was humiliated."

By now, several jurors were ready to hang Steve from the courthouse rafters, but Vogel wasn't finished. It was time to re-enact the crime:

"Penny, what I'd like to do is just have you get up out of your chair," Vogel started, "Mr. Beerntsen, why don't you come up here, can you do that? What I'd like to do is go back and have you show the jury a couple things in terms of how

59

you were grabbed. Have your husband grab onto you, have him take his arms or whatever and show how you were first grabbed as you were jogging."

With the spellbound jury looking on, Penny gave instructions to her husband: "Put your right arm there and your left arm here."

"Okay, initially his hand was on my shoulder," Penny explained, "When I twisted to holler to the sailboat, he did exactly what my husband just did. He grabbed my neck and cut off my windpipe … you can let go now."

Vogel awkwardly chimed in: "For the record, you're demonstrating your husband has his left arm around you, his right hand would be on your right arm, is that a fair statement?"

"That's correct," Penny answered.

"Show me how you were being held when you were half-way into the woods," Vogel asked, "when the top of your bikini was removed."

"Okay," Penny started, "with this arm, okay, he removed his left hand and then undid, I don't know, the top or the back first. At this point I twisted. He again put his left arm around my neck and said, 'Do what I tell you, I've got a knife'."

Then, summoning up his most official sounding prosecutorial voice, Vogel pronounced that "the record should reflect a similar grasp is being shown, except there was some release of the left arm momentarily."

If the jury thought this was preposterous, they didn't voice their distaste on the record, but Vogel continued:

"When you were in the wooded area, or close to the wooded area, you told us about the conversation about touching his penis and so forth. Could you just show me in which position you were at that time?"

"Okay, we were face-to-face."

"Penny, turn the other way so we can both see. Can you see, Mr. Bolgert?"

Redirecting his attention to Penny now, "You indicated before that you did touch his penis – how did you do that?"

"With my right hand," Penny explained.

Vogel mercifully moved on: "You indicated he pushed you down on the ground – show me how he did that."

Penny directed her husband to grab lower on her shoulders and then she replied, "He grabbed both my shoulders like this, okay? My arms were pressed against my body, and then he pushed me down onto the ground."

"Okay, can we just slowly do that? How was he over you? That's what I want to know."

"Okay, I was lying on my back like this."

"Can everybody see okay?" Vogel asked the jury, "If you can't see, stand up."

Penny instructed her husband to move his knees back a little further, and then Vogel asked her if the assailant's pants were still open and his penis exposed.

Penny replied in the affirmative. And then, thank goodness, it was finished. Vogel terminated the re-enactment, and Penny returned to the stand.

* * *

So far, Vogel had placed two separate renditions of the crime before the jury and now it was time for number three. A few days after the assault, Sheriff Kocourek met the Beerntsens at Neshotah Park and took dozens of photographs of the crime scene. After a few strings were pulled, a Coast Guard helicopter even snapped a few from the sky. Now, with Penny still on the stand, Vogel wanted to show some of those photos to the jury:

"I'm showing you what's been marked as Exhibit 9," he started, "Do you recognize that?"

'Yes," Penny answered, "it's a photo of the area of Neshotah Beach. This is the tree where my assailant was standing. I'm looking northbound here."

"How about Exhibit 10?"

"That's a close up of the tree, looking north."

"Exhibit 11?"

"The same tree, only this time looking south."

"12?"

"That's the same area of the beach with the tree, looking southbound. I'm standing in the water approximately at that point where I began to jog into the water. My husband is standing in the shadow of the tree where Mr. Avery was standing."

Vogel continued, rapidly now:

"What's Exhibit 8?"

"The incline of the sand dune area that Mr. Avery pushed me up."

"12?"

"Okay, this is a picture of the wooded area where I was assaulted, and I'm standing approximately on the spot where the assault occurred."

"14?"

"This is a close-up of the wooded area where I was assaulted – I'm standing on the spot where I was assaulted, where I was lying on the ground."

It was all very interesting, but it had virtually nothing to do with what the jury would have to decide, which was whether Steven Avery was the assailant. That Penny Beerntsen was brutally assaulted, and where the attack occurred was not contested. The only issue was: who did it?

But Vogel had beaten the dead horse for a reason. Relying almost entirely on the victim's dicey identification in the face of an impressive alibi by the defense – even if the unsavory Averys were the ones claiming the alibi – the prosecution's case was weak. And if you don't have the goods as far as the evidence goes, your best shot is to play on the jury's emotions. Prosecutors aren't supposed to play this game, but that didn't stop Vogel. By placing the brutal details of the assault in front of the jury no less than three separate times, he played on the jury's emotions, and his performance went off almost flawlessly.

But after awhile, even the most tough-on-crime jurors sense prosecutorial overreaching, and no matter how vicious the crime or how sympathetic the victim, at some point they start demanding proof. So it was finally time for Vogel to move beyond the viciousness of the assault to proof that the defendant was the person who committed it. Without a confession or any legitimate physical evidence tying Steven Avery to the crime, the prosecution relied almost exclusively on Penny's identification – it was the lynchpin of the State's case. The prosecution had to show that the identification was rock solid and unimpeachable.

Vogel set the scene by having Penny describe how Chief Deputy Gene Kusche came into her hospital room and worked with her to create a composite sketch of her assailant. Then he led his witness: "This is important now, Penny. At any time did Deputy Kusche suggest to you any of the features that might appear on your assailant?"

"No, no, not at all," Penny answered.

"Were you the one making the suggestions to him as to what the features look like?"

"Yes."

"In other words, the changes he may have made on that drawing, how were those changes directed, by himself making those decisions, or by you telling him to make the changes?"

"No, by me telling him to make the changes," Penny replied.

In preparation for the trial, Vogel had enlarged the mug shot of Avery that Penny picked out from the photo array at the hospital that night. Now, he directed her to get up from the witness stand and walk over to the enlargement where he resumed leading his witness: "Is this the picture that you picked out in that photo lineup without anybody telling you what your assailant would look like, or that he might be in the lineup, that sort of thing?"

"Yes, that's the picture."

Then he asked a question that together with Penny's response would years later echo with irony: "Did you have a picture in your mind, Penny?"

"Yes, I remembered very clearly," Penny answered, "It's as if there's a photograph in my mind."

A convincing courtroom identification by the victim is essential in a close case like this one, so Vogel summoned up as much drama as he could and led Penny through the prosecution's standard questions for a courtroom ID:

Would you recognize the person that attacked you if you saw that person today?"

Yes," Penny replied.

"Is that person in the courtroom right now?"

"Yes, he is."

"Can you please tell me where?"

"Yes. He's seated next to Mr. Bolgert in the tan suit."

Judge Hazlewood interjected, "The record will reflect identification."

But the prosecutor wanted to get as much mileage as he could from Penny's ID, so he went on: "Looking at Mr. Avery today, the defendant, do you understand that your ability to be positive about your assailant is important in this case?"

"Yes, I do."

"Have you thought about that from the time when this case began, when you actually became involved in the process until today's trial, have you thought about how important that is?"

"Yes, I have."

"Penny, is there any question in your mind as to whether or not the person you picked out for us today is in fact the person that attacked you?"

"There is absolutely no question in my mind."

Vogel's timing couldn't have been better. Vogel had come out of the blocks strong. The last thing the jurors would have on their minds as they broke for lunch was Penny's dramatic courtroom identification of Avery as her assailant. If you'll forgive the mixed metaphor, he'd hit a homerun.

But it was only the first morning of a trial that was expected to last a full week, so before excusing the jurors for lunch, Judge Hazlewood reminded them that they hadn't heard the whole case yet: "It's much too early to begin discussing the evidence or to begin your deliberations," he warned, "so please don't discuss the case during your lunch break."

But with Penny Beerntsen's harrowing testimony about the assault and her surefire identification of the defendant as the assailant, some of the jurors were already convinced that Steve was the culprit. Sure, they'd officially wait until they heard all the testimony to convict him, but Jim Bolgert would need to play some extremely scrappy defense in the afternoon to avert a blowout. If he didn't, they might just as well serve Avery's head on a platter for the jury's dinner that night.

It's Trial Practice 101. There are two things to remember for effective cross-examination: first, never ask a question if you don't know the answer; and second, don't beat around the bush – get in and out quickly. Jim Bolgert did well on both counts that afternoon.

With his bright blue-eyed client sitting beside him at counsel table, he fired off his first question: "Ms. Beerntsen, did your attacker have brown eyes?"

"I originally said he had brown eyes," Penny admitted, "but when I picked him out of the photo line-up, I handed it to the Sheriff and said, 'He's got blue eyes – I was mistaken'."

"And you also told Deputy Dvorak two days later that he had brown eyes, is that correct?"

"That's correct."

"And you were speaking from your memory when you told Deputy Dvorak that?"

"Yes."

"And you were being truthful?"

"Yes."

Then Bolgert stepped in for another jab. He'd mentioned in his opening statement that his client worked on cars for a living so his hands were always greasy, and with Penny on the stand now, he asked her if the assailant's hands were greasy. The jury's collective ears perked up as Penny responded: "No, they were clean."

Bolgert finished up with another question or two and then turned it back over to the prosecution. Vogel tried to repair the damage during re-direct examination, but the point had been made and it was impossible to un-ring the bell.

With Penny's testimony completed, Vogel called his second witness – the emergency room physician who treated her on the night of the assault. If a picture's worth a thousand words, then showing a gruesome photograph to a jury is worth millions. So it's not surprising that the first spat between the lawyers began when Vogel tried to introduce a particularly grisly photograph taken in the emergency room that night – a photo that showed Penny's face beaten to a bloody pulp.

Arguing that the probative value of the photo was, "substantially outweighed by the danger of unfair prejudice," as the evidence code puts it, Jim Bolgert objected on relevance grounds. The issue isn't how badly the victim was beaten, he argued, it's who committed this brutal assault. The photograph appeals to sympathy for the victim and disgust for whoever assaulted her – that's the only reason the State wants it in front of the jury, Judge.

But that's not how Denis Vogel saw it: "I don't believe there's any better way to show the nature and extent of the victim's beating than using the photographs," he professed. "The extent of the beating is critical in this case, and this photograph corroborates it, it corroborates the victim's testimony."

Noting that one of the charges was attempted murder, Judge Hazlewood agreed: "With respect to the photographs of the injuries, the Court believes they're reasonable and valuable evidence to the jury, and while they're not exactly the most pleasant things to look at, I believe it's reasonably necessary for the State to use those photographs to demonstrate the nature and extent of the attack. Therefore, the objection is overruled."

The floodgates were open. "I'm showing you what's been marked as Exhibit 1," Vogel announced, more to the jury than the emergency room physician to whom he'd addressed the question, "Is this a photograph of the way Penny looked when you saw her at the hospital that night?"

"Yes, it is," the ER doc replied.

Vogel asked the Judge if he could publish the oversized photograph to the jury. The Court approved, and Vogel strutted slowly along the front of the jury box, pausing before each juror just long enough to give them a good look at the photograph of Penny in his hands.

Back at counsel table, Vogel continued: "Do you have an opinion to a reasonable degree of scientific certainty, doctor, as to whether or not the bruise at the base of Penny's neck would be consistent with someone choking her?"

"It very well could have been."

"The degree of force required, doctor, to cause that sort of bruising, do you have an opinion to a reasonable degree of scientific certainty as to the amount of force required to cause that?"

"It's relatively hard to cause the breaking of the blood vessels there to cause that kind of bruising."

"Do you have an opinion to a reasonable degree of scientific certainty as to how much force would be required to cause bruising to her back the way you saw it, to a reasonable scientific certainty, that it would be consistent with Penny being shaken or pushed on the ground up and down several times?"

"Could very well have been, yes," the ER doctor mildly replied.

As his next witness, Vogel called Sherry Culhane from the State Crime Lab in Madison. Among other things, Culhane and the other analysts at the Crime Lab examine biological evidence – hair, blood, semen, saliva, that sort of thing – in an attempt to identify their source, which is often a key piece of evidence in solving a crime. But back in 1985 the science of hair examination, if it could even be called a science, was extremely limited. It was ten years before the advent of forensic DNA testing, and with the tools available at the time, hair examiners couldn't even come close to making a positive identification – the best they could do was to say that two hairs were "consistent."

The police had confiscated Steve's tee-shirt on the night of the assault, and Culhane had collected various hairs from it. One of the hairs was a possible match with the standard hair provided by Penny Beerntsen, but all Culhane could say is that the two hairs were similar. But as dutifully elicited by Vogel, at least her opinion was "to a reasonable degree of scientific certainty."

Jim Bolgert destroyed the "science" of hair examination during cross-examination, and to her credit, Sherry Culhane didn't try to make hair examination sound more useful than it was.

"Is it possible to prove identification by hair analysis?" Bolgert began.

"No."

"Is the hair of many people consistent with each other?"

"Yes."

"Is it unusual for hair from different people to be consistent with each other?"

"No, it's not."

"For example, is it unusual for the hair of white Caucasians to be consistent with each other?"

"No."

"If you take a hair from ten different people, would it be unusual to find the hair from those different people to be consistent?"

"No."

"Did you have any standards from hospital or ambulance personnel?"

"No, sir."

"Did you have any standards from the husband of the victim?"

"No, sir."

"Any standards from any of Mr. Avery's children?"

"No, sir."

* * *

The cops came next. Vogel called four in a row to establish that it was none other than the defendant himself who the police arrested that night for this despicable crime. Sergeant Petersen explained that with the assistance of the defendant's uncle, Deputy Arland Avery, they were able to take the "subject" into custody without incident.

Then, out came the smoking gun. Two officers testified that the defendant knew the victim was a woman even though nobody told him. Sergeant Petersen was the first to drop the bomb:

"What happened next?" Vogel asked.

"The defendant's wife came downstairs and asked him what was going on, and he said, 'They say I murdered a woman'."

"Did he use the word 'woman'?" Vogel asked, to make sure the jury appreciated the weight of the moment.

"Yes," Petersen replied.

"Prior to that time, you hadn't mentioned the word 'woman' when you arrested him, had you?"

"No, not at all."

"Had anyone else mentioned that it was a woman?"

"Not in my presence."

Then it was Deputy Froelich's turn. First, he explained how he hid in a closet until the defendant came downstairs and then followed him into the kitchen where he and Sergeant Petersen arrested him.

Vogel took it from there: "When the defendant's wife came downstairs, did she ask him anything?"

"His wife asked, 'would somebody please tell me what's going on?' and then Sergeant Petersen and myself, we just looked at each other, and Steve – Steve looked at his wife and said, 'They said I murdered a girl'."

"When he said that, did you specifically make note of that, a mental note that he said it?"

"Yes."

Then Vogel went in for the kill: "Why?"

"Because at that point, no one had said it was a male or female."

Penny Beerntsen told the police several times that the assailant was wearing a worn-out waist length black leather jacket. But since black leather jackets aren't uncommon, neither party made much of it until miraculously just three days before trial, when Vogel sent word to the defense. He disclosed that over the years, Deputies Froelich and Dvorak had both seen the defendant wearing a black leather jacket. As a matter of fact, it was just like the one Penny described.

Now, with Froelich still on the stand, Vogel asked him about the jacket: "Prior to July 29, 1985, had you ever seen Mr. Avery wearing any sort of a leather jacket?"

"Yes," Froelich replied.

"More than one time?"

"Yes, it's a black waist length motorcycle type leather jacket."

"Is that an old looking jacket to your knowledge?" Vogel asked, leading his witness.

"Yes, old looking," Froelich parroted the prosecutor.

"Are there any specific dates or times you remember specifically seeing him having that jacket?"

"Yes."

Then Froelich pulled out a copy of a child safety-seat warning that he'd issued Avery on April 6, 1984 and handed it to Vogel.

"For example," Vogel continued, holding up the warning, "on this particular date and time, do you remember what Steve was wearing?"

"He was wearing the black, faded black, motorcycle jacket. And I've seen him wearing the jacket more recently, but I just don't remember any specific dates."

But nobody other than one other officer, Deputy Judy Dvorak, testified that they ever saw Steve with a black leather jacket like Penny's assailant had on, and when they executed the search warrant at Steve and Lori's house the morning after the attack, the police didn't find one either. Also, despite seeing him every week for as long as he could remember, deputy Arland Avery, Steve's uncle, never saw him wearing any leather jacket – not once. Vogel later called Arland to the stand, but conveniently, he didn't ask him if he ever saw his nephew wearing a leather jacket.

When Vogel called Judy Dvorak next, the lawyers had their second spat – and it was a good one. The fireworks started when halfway through direct examination, Vogel asked Deputy Dvorak to read out loud Penny's entire six-page statement. A few days had passed since Penny's dramatic testimony, and its effect on the jury was probably wearing off. It would help immensely, Vogel thought, if he could get the brutal assault back in the forefront of their minds.

Bolgert objected – and then all hell broke loose. Spewing out legal concepts like hearsay, prior inconsistent statements, and implied allegations of recent fabrication, the attorneys snarled at each other and gnashed their teeth. Then the Judge stepped in to clear the air:

"How much more are we going to hear about this statement? How many times should we be re-reading these statements is almost a battle of who gets the last kick at the cat, this kind of an argument I'm hearing. I'm beginning to think this is just wasting a lot of time."

Vogel unwisely interrupted, "Judge, I agree with what you're saying – at some point in time you might hear too much, and we want to get on with other witnesses."

Judge Hazlewood dryly cut him off, "We sure would."

Nobody was left standing in the end, but the Judge eventually gave in and Vogel got what he wanted. He had Deputy Dvorak read Penny's riveting six–page statement – reminding the jurors once again of the viciousness of the assault, lest they start to think the State's case was less than convincing.

Vogel was delighted, but during his cross-examination, Jim Bolgert came back strong. "You stated after that statement was signed, that Penny changed her description of the eyes from brown eyes to blue, isn't that right?"

"Yes," Dvorak admitted, "it was not noted on the statement."

"Did that happen the same day or is that on your interview of August 1?"

"I believe this is what she told the Sheriff, possibly that first evening."

"Did she ever tell you the attacker had blue eyes?"

"Yes, after I had taken the second statement."

"On August 1st?"

"Yes."

Bolgert continued: "So the first time she told you about the blue eyes was on August 1 – three days after the assault?"

"Yes."

Then he shifted gears and scored a few more blows while he still had Dvorak on the stand: "Deputy Dvorak, did you specifically ask Ms. Beerntsen whether the attacker's hands were dirty or greasy?"

"Yes, I did," Dvorak answered softly, "and she did not include any mention of them being greasy or dirty."

He let her response sink in, and then he moved on: "You don't know if Steven Avery owns a leather jacket like the assailant was wearing, do you?"

"No, but I have seen him with an older looking dark leather jacket."

Noting vagueness, and suspecting disingenuousness, Bolgert honed in: "When is the most recent time?"

"I couldn't be sure," Dvorak backtracked, "but I remember last Fall I had seen him wearing it several times, and during the winter."

"Where did you see him?"

"Steve lives across Old County Hwy Y from where I live. Our residence is just to the east on the opposite side of the road."

"So you would see him when you drove by occasionally, is that when you'd see him?"

"I would see him in the yard as I walked by, or I jog frequently, or when I do walk, when I drive by, yes," Dvorak babbled.

"Was there any reason for you to take note of what he was wearing?"

"Not really. I also have the project child safe car, the safe car-seat project, and I had to pick up a car-seat from Steve once in his home also."

"He was wearing that coat?"

"I can't be sure on that, but I believe he may have been."

"But you had no particular reason to remember what he was wearing, did you?"

"No, I did not."

"Did you make notes when you saw him wearing different items of clothing?"

"No, I did not," Dvorak said defensively, "this is not a thing you generally do about your neighbors."

Bolgert deadpanned, "I agree," and then he wrapped it up: "Were you specifically asked whether you had ever seen Steve wearing a short leather coat for the purpose of this case?"

"Yes," Dvorak said vaguely, "it has come out in a conversation."

Vogel's next witness was Chief Deputy Gene Kusche (pronounced *Kushay*). He began with the prosecutor's standard "would-you-please-state-your-name-and-occupation" question, and Kusche, and as he did everything in life, Kusche replied with a flourish: "I am Eugene Kusche, Chief Deputy Sheriff for Manitowoc County."

Kusche had attended the FBI Academy just a month before Penny was assaulted, and Vogel asked him if the training included eye-witness identification procedure and police artist reconstruction.

"Yes," the Chief Deputy responded, "I attended a course in what's called rapid visual perception. It's on how to train individuals, such as bank clerks or what-have-you, on what to look for in facial characteristics. Part of the course was also on how to prepare the drawing, the composite comparisons."

Then, sounding uncharacteristically defensive, Vogel set the stage for Kusche's drawing of the composite sketch:

"In this particular case, did you have any suspects in mind before you made the drawing for Penny Beerntsen?"

"Did I have in *my* mind?" Kusche responded with a question of his own.

"Yes," Vogel answered.

"Visually?" Kusche asked.

"Yes, visually or any other way," the prosecutor replied.

"I was told a name earlier, but I did not know the person," Kusche finally answered.

Then Vogel led with a mouthful: "So you had no preconceived ideas of your own of any particular features or any drawings or any descriptions of anybody prior to talking to Penny Beerntsen?" And just in case the jury didn't get the picture, he continued: "So you're saying you didn't see any photographs and neither did the victim, is that correct?"

"I did not, and to my knowledge the victim did not," Kusche answered, catching on, with more certainty this time.

"At any time during your interview of Penny," Vogel continued, "did anyone come in and suggest to you a name or a description?"

"Not a description, I know a name was stated to me," Kusche answered, "but I don't know if she was within earshot at the time it was stated to me."

Vogel moved on: "Now, once you had the victim at ease and began the interview, did you suggest any features of a face to the victim?"

"No, sir. You ask them to tell you, then you draw what you think they mean and if it is not, like I said, they will correct it, and one of the important portions of the training is not to be suggestive, like you don't say, 'Did the person have a round face?' Instead, you ask 'What was the shape of the face?', so that way," Kusche said, *"you're not putting anything in their mind.* (emphasis added)*"*

Then it was time to present the artist with his masterpiece: "I show you what's been marked as Exhibit Number 26," Vogel confidently declared, "and I ask if you recognize it?"

"This is my original drawing – the charcoal drawing."

"Is Exhibit Number 26 the final product?"

"It is," Kusche said, "this was the original and final drawing."

Sensing that the prosecution had scored a few points for the defense, or at least that they'd turned the ball over a few times, Jim Bolgert kept his cross-examination short and sweet.

"You mentioned that the mug shots for the photo lineup had been pulled before the composite was done. Is that standard practice?" he began.

"Apparently from the description prior to me arriving at the scene or at the hospital, the officers had some idea of who it might be. Therefore, it would not be unusual that photographs would be pulled," Kusche replied.

"Did she give you a description of eye color?"

"I can't say that I asked," Kusche demurred, "so I don't remember that."

"That wouldn't be part of your standard procedure, to ask eye color?"

"It would probably be, but in this case I can't recollect having asked her. I may have, but as I did not do this in color I didn't make any representation in color."

By being so adamantly defensive about whether their immediate suspicion of Avery affected the integrity of the composite drawing and the identification process itself, the prosecution invited speculation that it had done just that. Indeed, both the composite drawing and Avery's mug shot, marked as exhibits 22 and 26 respectively, figured prominently in the trial, and over the years more than a few persons who've seen them have commented that the composite drawing looks *exactly* like Avery's mug shot. Indeed, Judge Hazlewood, himself, referred to the two depictions as bearing an "uncanny resemblance" to each other.

The composite sketch drawn by Eugene Kusche

* * *

Both lawyers knew it. If Steven Avery attacked Penny Beerntsen on the beach that afternoon, he had to move fast. For Penny was as precise about the time of the assault as she was sketchy about the assailant's appearance – she checked her watch when she first saw the man hiding in the poplar trees, and it was ten minutes to four.

But Avery and his family were adamant that Steve came into the house right after *Divorce Court* ended at three-thirty. That would leave him just twenty minutes to drive to Neshotah Beach and position himself under the poplar tree ready to pounce on his prey. It's a fifteen minute drive from the Avery Salvage Yard to Neshotah Park, which would him leave just five minutes to park and shuffle a half mile up the sand to the poplar trees – it was close to impossible.

Vogel's ace in the hole was the cement truck driver, Donald Cigler. Steve's wife, his mother, and various other members of the Avery clan all told police the cement truck was still there when Steve came in after *Divorce Court* ended at three-thirty. But that's not how Cigler remembered it. He testified he arrived at one o'clock that afternoon with ten yards of concrete. Then Vogel asked him what time he left, and Cigler took it from there:

"Well, they poured a slab for a sheep barn, and then they had some small odd pours around the building. I must have left around two-thirty I'd say – somewheres in there. Then I went back to the pit. It's about five or six miles back to the pit. When I got back to the pit, I washed up the truck with some water in there and then dumped that, parked it, and shut it off. It takes about ten minutes or so to wash the truck, so I estimate it was half an hour after I left the Averys' that I checked out and went home. We have timecards that we fill out ourselves, and on that date I entered seven and a half hours, so since I began work at seven-thirty and worked right through noon without a lunch hour, that means I checked out at three. So I'd say it was around two-thirty when I left the Avery place."

If the cement truck left at two-thirty like Donald Cigler said it did, then either the defense witnesses were mistaken or they were lying. It also meant that Steve finished helping with the cement project much earlier than he claimed and he would have had plenty of time to drive to Neshotah Park and be in position to attack Penny at ten minutes to four.

During cross-examination, Bolgert established that Cigler worked different hours each day and that he didn't punch out on a time clock – he kept track of his hours in a notebook he kept at home instead. And no, he didn't tell his boss how many hours he worked that day.

Nevertheless, Donald Cigler probably saved the prosecution. In his round-about way, he laid out a time frame that made it possible for Steven Avery to be at the scene of the crime at the time Penny was attacked. Never mind that years later, a private investigator would discover that Cigler was overheard saying as he left the courtroom that day that "I think I'd gypped myself out of an hour."

* * *

The prosecution also had to come up with a credible time-line for what Steve did after the assault, and the window of opportunity wasn't open much wider on that side of the equation. Penny said the assault lasted fifteen minutes and ended at approximately 4:05. But Steve and his family were in the checkout lane at ShopKo in Green Bay at 5:13. To make it on time, he would've had to run from the crime scene back to where he parked his Blazer, hustle back to his parents' place to pick up his wife and five children, and then drive thirty miles up the Interstate to Green Bay – all in sixty-eight minutes! It was nearly impossible.

Not to worry. A few days after Penny was assaulted, Detective Fred Nicholson conducted a dry run to see how long it would have taken the assailant to get from the scene of the crime to the checkout line at ShopKo in Green Bay. Nicholson told the jury that by intermittently running and walking at a fast pace, it took him thirteen minutes to get from where Duke the police dog found Penny's bathing suit to the public parking lot at Neshotah Beach. And "averaging fifteen miles per hour over the limit, but never more than fifteen over," it took another forty-four minutes to drive to Shopko, grab a gallon of paint, and walk to the checkout lane. Fifty-seven minutes total – he made it with eleven minutes to spare!

Detective Nicholson's math was fine, but he left a few numbers out of the equation. He didn't count the time it would have taken Steve to pick up Lori and the kids, including two who were infants. Nor the time they spent at the Burger King Drive-Thru and the car wash across the street.

Hoping to finish strong, Vogel called Sheriff Kocourek as his final witness. "Could you please tell everyone what your occupation is?" he began.

"Sheriff of Manitowoc County," Kocourek replied.

"And were you involved in coordinating the investigation of the incident regarding Penny Beerntsen?"

"Yes."

"When you presented the photo array to her, did you lay them out for her, or just give her a stack to finger through?"

"I just spread them out on a table and she looked at all of them at the same time."

"And did Penny Beerntsen pick out any one of those photographs for you?"

"Yes, she did."

"Which one did she pick?"

"She picked out photograph number 3746, which is of Steven Avery," the Sheriff answered.

"Was there any hesitancy that you could observe about her when she was asked to pick out a photograph and when she did in fact pick out that photograph?"

Kocourek replied in his measured, convincing voice that he didn't detect any hesitancy. "As a matter of fact," he said, "I noted that she was kind of drawn to that one, and then she sort of held her hand on this one and looked at the others – but then she came right back to this one and said, 'This is the man.'"

Though flawed, like the rest of us are, Tom Kocourek is a man of high ideals and solid integrity, and his testimony during Jim Bolgert's cross-examination bears that out. There's no doubt about it – the Sheriff took his oath seriously:

"Before July 29, did you know Steve?" Bolgert began.

"Yes, I did."

"And that was through professional contacts?"

"That's correct."

"When you heard that description, you suspected Steve?"

"Yes."

"And did you tell the victim that you had a suspect in mind?"

"Yes."

"Did you instruct your deputies to pull some photographs?"

"Yes."

"And did you instruct them to include a few mug shots of Steven Avery?"

"Yes."

"When did you do that?"

"It would have been during the evening of July 29."

"Before the composite was drawn?"

"Yes."

"Did you have those photos before you," Bolgert continued, "before the composite was drawn?"

"They were delivered to me at the hospital," the Sheriff replied.

"Before the composite was drawn, did you indicate to the artist that you had a suspect in mind?"

"Yes."

"When the composite was done, did you immediately present the photographs to her?"

"After the composite was complete and she was sure in her mind that there wasn't much more that she could offer to, you know, change the composite, the composite was set aside and the photographs were presented to her."

"Do you think she realized that those photos had been pulled before the composite was drawn?"

"I'm sure she probably did, yes," the Sheriff replied.

Then Bolgert switched gears and finished up crisply: "The other times you've seen Steven Avery, did you ever see him wearing a waist length leather jacket?"

"No."

"That's all I have, thank you."

"Any redirect, Mr. Vogel?" Judge Hazlewood invited.

Vogel's barely audible reply was a curt, "No."

"Mr. Vogel, anything else?" the Court repeated.

"No, Your Honor; the State rests."

Jim Bolgert had come back strong and, for once, Denis Vogel had nothing to say.

The prosecution had called twenty-one witnesses and offered forty-nine exhibits into evidence, and now it was finally time for the case to pass to the defense. Even though there was time for a witness or two, Judge Hazlewood decided to call it a day. The defense could start fresh in the morning that way – and besides, it had turned ugly outside. The first cold snap of the year had descended upon Wisconsin, and with a few of the older jurors getting nervous, Judge Fred tried to put them at ease:

> "Some of you expressed concerns about your automobiles. If you're concerned about the cars not starting, or if you'd like someone to start up your car or something like that, perhaps we could collect the keys tomorrow morning, and we could have people out starting the cars and turning them over. It hasn't been real cold in the evening, so if the car's in good winter condition, it probably should start, but we'll check."

With the State's case in, and the defense ready to take over the reins the following morning, the Judge finished by reminding the jury not to begin deliberating until they heard all the evidence:

> "I know the temptation is tremendous to sit down and start trying to decide the case, but there's still more evidence to come, so don't begin your deliberations at this time. Hopefully we can provide you with a good dinner – I haven't heard any complaints yet – that's always a good sign. I thank you for the attention that you've given to me and to counsel today. At this point we're adjourning. Thank you, ladies and gentlemen."

TEN

IT'S CUSTOMARY, and almost universally a waste of time, for the defense to ask the Court to dismiss the charges after the State rests its case. Not to do so is to risk a claim of ineffective assistance of counsel. So with both counsel and the defendant present in chambers, Judge Hazlewood asked if the defense had a motion, and Jim Bolgert dutifully, if unenthusiastically, replied: "I'd move to dismiss on the grounds the State hasn't met its burden of proof, Your Honor."

Still following the script, Judge Hazlewood invoked the equally meaningless legal standard for such matters and efficiently dispatched of the motion: "Based upon the testimony in the record at this time, the Court is satisfied that a reasonable jury could find beyond a reasonable doubt that the defendant is guilty. The Court therefore respectfully denies the Motion."

The term "reasonable" shows up often in the law. It allows for plenty of wiggle room since to some extent, whether something is reasonable is in the eye of the beholder.

It was the moment the Averys had been waiting for. In the five and a half months since Steve's arrest, they had lost what little faith they previously held in the criminal justice system. But once the facts were placed before a jury of their peers, they thought, justice would surely prevail. How couldn't it? Steve was innocent – he was with them all day.

As his first witness, Jim Bolgert planned to call Dr. Steven Penrod, a highly regarded expert in human memory and eyewitness identification procedures from the University of Wisconsin in Madison. Given how the police extracted his client's identification from the victim in this case, Bolgert knew that Penrod would make an excellent witness, and somehow he managed to convince the State Public Defender's Office to approve his fee.

But Denis Vogel tried to head him off at the pass. He moved to exclude much of Dr. Penrod's proffered testimony on the grounds that it would invade the province of the jury. On its surface, at least, the law seems fairly simple: unless there's a question of fact that is "beyond the scope of ordinary lay persons' knowledge and experience," testimony from expert witnesses is inadmissible at trial. The jurors are the finders of fact – not some expert witness retained by one side or the other at some exorbitant fee.

But applying the law is rarely straightforward, and after Vogel objected, Judge Hazlewood launched into a lengthy discussion about whether Dr. Penrod should be allowed to testify.

"Turning now to the issue of the identification expert, Dr. Steven Penrod," the Judge began, "I've indicated to counsel that the Court would permit testimony of a properly qualified expert – and I do not at this time mean to imply that I have a feeling one way or the other with regard to Mr. Penrod's qualifications – I presume we'll hear more about that on the record. But perhaps I better hear the State's objection to the proffered testimony. And perhaps before we even hear the State's objection, we'd better hear what the defense expects to do with the testimony."

"Your Honor, the expert's name is Steven Penrod, and there's no doubt in my mind he's qualified," Bolgert replied. "After his qualifications, I'm going to ask him to speak about the area of human memory and eyewitness identification. He speaks of memory as having four stages: perception; encoding; storage; and retrieval. I'll ask him to explain each. As you know from my questions on cross, there are specific elements of the identification I'd like to ask him about – specifically, the effect upon the victim of assuming the Sheriff had a suspect and that he was in the array; the effect of confirmation of her choice and the subsequent arrest; the effect of her knowledge of the person who was arrested and in custody before the live lineup; the confirmation that she picked the suspect after the live lineup; and later information that this person had some prior contact with law enforcement. With the Court's permission, I'd also show him the photo lineup, and not ask for his opinion, but to critique it as a functional array."

At that, Vogel jumped in: "What Mr. Bolgert wants to do has been accepted, Judge, but not to the extent he wants to have it applied in this case. What he wants to do is apply the general theory that Penrod apparently has of perception, encoding, the retention – or in his words, storage and retrieval – and then take that general theory and apply it specifically to the facts in this case and have him comment on the facts in this case but not get to the ultimate conclusion, that being do you think it's a good or bad identification. It's invading the province of the jury, Your Honor, and really, although he's not asking him the ultimate question, he is asking him to draw an opinion, and by going that far, the jury would draw the inference as to what his opinion is. I don't think it's admissible to go as far as Mr. Bolgert wants him to. I believe it would be an abuse of the Court's discretion to allow Penrod to do that, and that's the standard under the *Hampton* case – abuse of discretion."

Under what circumstances the Court should permit expert testimony concerning eye-witness identifications is the sort of thorny legal issue Judge Hazlewood relished, and now that the lawyers had their say, it was time for the Court to decide.

"This is an area of law that is causing us a great deal of trouble in the law," the Judge began, "and in recent years it's become a difficult matter to control, most critically in civil cases. But now it's become more a factor in criminal cases; that is, the place of the expert in the courtroom and whether or not the expert will, in effect, supersede the jury in reaching these determinations. Fundamentally, it's a question of where we place our confidence. Do we place our confidence in twelve persons from the community, or do we place it in listening to two experts? The thing I'm stricken with in many cases with regard to experts is how two persons with impeccable credentials, incredible academic efforts attested to by their many publications, and a great deal of practical experience in the field in which they testify, can come to diametrically opposed conclusions. I'm conservative, and I retain a considerable amount of faith in the jury system. I tend to believe that expert testimony is admissible only when it assists lay persons in reaching conclusions, and when the expert can provide, because of his expertise and experience, insights into matters that are relevant and that are beyond the pale of the average person to understand or appreciate fully."

Clearly enjoying the argument, which by now had turned one-sided, Judge Hazlewood continued: "The factors which affect memory and perception – I'm sure all of us have opinions on. I'm also certain that with respect to whatever opinions we may hold, and whatever beliefs we may hold, it is not necessarily going to adversely – and it could very well properly assist us – in applying not only our opinions but in considering them in light of the studied opinion of an expert in the area to a specific set of facts."

"I am unwilling, however, to allow experts in the field of identification to comment or to testify on the deficiencies of a particular identification in particular situations, or give an opinion on the reliability of that particular identification. I do not have any basis to believe that the fields of psychology and psychiatry have reached such a point where one can reliably put in the hands of psychiatrists and psychologists or other persons specifically trained in these areas the task of reaching the conclusion that the jury will be reaching."

"Now, when we say ultimate issue, the ultimate issue is the guilt or innocence of the defendant. But in getting to that stage, there are many other decisions that, absent some considerable proof that this area of science has arrived at a consistent opinion that would remove the matter from the area of the lay person's application of wisdom and logic, are properly left to the jury. Therefore, I believe the expert should be permitted to testify in this instance. However, I do not believe it is proper to ask him questions that go to the quality or the deficiencies of the identification process in this particular case, or to offer a critique, if you will, of the photo line-up or the live line-up."

It sounded like the Court was finished, but Judge Hazlewood had one last point: "I would add, by way of editorial comment, that certainly psychiatric testimony and psychological testimony is one area where people with incredible credentials come into Court with diametrically opposed opinions on the critical facts. And again, I would pose the same question of whether these two people – and whatever can be gleaned from that academic debate in the courtroom – is ultimately the better one, or whether that should be left to twelve people. I don't know."

Judge Hazlewood asked the bailiff to bring in the jury. The legal wrangling over the admission of expert testimony had gone on for nearly an hour, but the Judge greeted the jurors with his usual good cheer. He also had a comment about the weather outside, as the temperature had dropped to well below zero:

"In light of the control over the news broadcasts, some of you may have missed the weather report. It's getting much colder, so if any of you want your cars started or turned over, why don't you make arrangements to leave your keys with the bailiff with a license number, and we'll try to accomplish that for you today. And if the car won't start, we'll make arrangements to have the appropriate starter devices here and people to assist you in getting your car started. It's gotten quite cold."

Then he addressed the delay:

"Also, I don't want you to get the idea that because we're starting after nine o'clock that we're all drifting in here late in the morning and having long breakfasts while you're ready to go. There are numerous details that have to be dealt with in any jury trial, and it's difficult to predict how long these will take when the judge – who is supposed to know everything – has to nonetheless open a book and look at some law, as happens from time to time. I can assure you, counsel have been arriving promptly at eight-thirty. I can't assure you the Court got here quite at eight-thirty today – I was about three minutes late. But we're trying not to waste your time."

* * *

It was finally time for Dr. Penrod to take the stand. "How are you employed?" Bolgert began.

"I'm a professor of psychology at the University of Wisconsin in Madison."

"What's your educational background?"

"I have a bachelor's degree from Yale in 1969," Penrod replied, "and I have a law degree from Harvard Law School in 1974, and a PhD in psychology from Harvard University in 1979."

"Where were you employed prior to the University of Wisconsin, Dr. Penrod?

"I was a graduate student at Harvard University where I was employed as a teaching and research assistant. Prior to that time, I was in the Navy – I worked as a legal officer in the Navy, and I had various other and sundry jobs before that."

"What are your duties at the University of Wisconsin?"

"First would be teaching, second would be research, and third would be administrative responsibilities. Most of my research is conducted in areas where psychology and law intersect. I draw upon both of my sources of training for that research. At the moment, my primary research activities are focused on issues concerning eyewitness reliability, problems of eyewitness identification, and methods that might be used to assess the reliability of eyewitness identification. A couple years ago, I conducted a series of seminars for the Madison Police Department on methods of investigation, interrogation of witnesses, and construction of lineups, problems of eyewitness identification."

Then Bolgert offered Dr. Penrod as an expert in the study of human memory and eyewitness identification, and the Court asked Vogel if he had any objection.

Vogel unwisely replied: "I believe he's stated his qualifications in terms of his background, but I'm not sure if he specifically qualified himself as an expert on ..."

Clearly impressed with Penrod's credentials, Judge Hazlewood cut him off: "Well, I can do with a yes or no."

"Yes," Vogel curtly replied.

"Thank you. The Court will receive further testimony from Mr. Penrod."

Trial attorneys love calling expert witnesses. It's a rare opportunity to ask open-ended questions and sit back while your witness does the heavy lifting. It's even more enjoyable if your expert not only knows his stuff, but also knows how to speak to the jury in terms they can understand. Steven Penrod excelled at both.

So moving on to the issue at hand, for his first substantive question Bolgert lobbed Penrod a fat pitch right over the plate: "Would you please tell the jury how human memory operates, Dr. Penrod?"

Penrod hit the ball squarely: "Most psychologists break human memory down into four stages. The first stage is perception, which just refers to the stage at which whatever sensory system we're using – I'll concentrate on our visual system – actually receives stimulation. In the case of the eye, it receives light. Stimulated by light, we pick up visual images. That's the perception stage. A second stage commonly discussed is the encoding stage. It really refers to the active processing in terms of thinking about the information that's perceived. The third stage is commonly referred to as the storage stage, or sometimes, the retention interval. It refers to the period of time between the perception and encoding of information and then the later effort to pull that information out of memory. And finally, the retrieval stage, which is that stage of trying to retrieve information out of memory. Now, the reason that we break them down into those stages is because in fact, different things are happening at those stages in terms of forming the memory, and the eyewitness is prone to a variety of errors or problems at each of those different stages."

Then Penrod zeroed in on what might have occurred in this case: "We also know that things can happen even while information is being stored. So even if the person starts out with a good, rich, solid memory for an event, that doesn't mean that at some later point in time they're going to be able to retrieve that information from memory in its original and pure, pristine form. The reason is that events that take place after, let's say a crime, events that take place after viewing a crime can change or distort the original memory, and what happens is that if people pick up information after the crime, that information can literally become part of their original memory. While information is sitting in the storage stage, it can undergo changes, or transformations, that in essence can destroy the original memory. We know, for example, there have been several studies on the effects of overhearing another person talk about the characteristics of the perpetrator. Let's say witnesses had seen a staged crime or a videotape of a crime, and later they hear somebody say, 'I think he has a mustache,' or, 'I think he has curly hair,' those characteristics, those pieces of information – and they're false information and they've been sort of set up by the researcher to see what effect it will have on the witnesses' memories – those pieces of false information can find their way into an individual witness' memories, and at a later point in time they are significantly more likely to misidentify an individual who has the mustache as the perpetrator when the original perpetrator didn't, or an individual who has curly hair when the original perpetrator didn't have curly hair. These effects can be produced in very subtle ways."

Bolgert looked up from his notes and briefly interjected: "I was going to ask – is that a conscious process?"

"Absolutely not," Dr. Penrod replied, "This is not something where people sort of intentionally take that information and now put it into their memory. It's something that happens unintentionally, and indeed the witnesses who display these kinds of effects are trying the best they can to make a totally accurate report, but these influences are very, very subtle, but can nonetheless have a very profound effect on the witness' memory, and in some sense, the most disturbing aspect of this is that it proves to be virtually impossible for a witness to somehow go back and restore or retrieve their original memory."

"You said the viewing of a photo lineup could change the original memory," Bolgert chimed in, "How is that?"

"Well," Dr. Penrod explained as he turned to face the jury, "because the information that is picked up after an event – but it's relevant to the event – in a sense now becomes intermingled with the original information. We don't know exactly what goes on in the brain that produces this effect, but what we do know is that post-event information seems to become mingled, intermingled with the information from the original event. It can in some instances literally displace it so that it's impossible to retrieve memory about the face of the original perpetrator because it's been supplanted, replaced by, pushed out by, or intermingled with information that's picked up from these photographs."

Bolgert interjected again: "This change in original memory, is that a conscious process?"

"No," Penrod replied, "Again, it's not a conscious process, and it's something that proves to be fairly difficult to prevent. Indeed, it's a common problem."

Bolgert moved on: "We're specifically interested, Dr. Penrod, in what effect expectation might have on a photo-identification."

"If a person has an expectation that the perpetrator is going to be there," Penrod explained, "it seems to change the identification task for them. Instead of having the sole responsibility for saying, well, out of these six possible suspects this is the person, and then the case proceeds solely on the basis of that identification, the task now seems to be one of confirming or disconfirming police suspicions and the thought is that if a misidentification occurs – if the wrong person is picked – there won't be any harm done. On the other hand, if I pick the same person that the police have picked, we'll have some corroborating identifications, if you will, so it seems to change the task and simply make people more willing to make identifications. They're just not as conservative about making their identifications."

Penny Beerntsen had testified confidently – she was absolutely certain the photo she picked out was her assailant, so Bolgert wrapped up his direct examination by asking Dr. Penrod whether there's a relationship between the accuracy of the identification and the confidence in the person that they've made a proper identification.

"Unfortunately not," Penrod answered, "and despite the fact that it defies common sense, there have been a large number of studies which show that if there is a relationship between confidence and accuracy, it's only a weak relationship. We just are not very good at sort of crawling inside our memory and trying to determine whether it's a good, solid memory or not so good a memory."

With that, Bolgert was finished and he passed his witness to the prosecution. Dr. Penrod's testimony was fascinating, but after nearly two hours of sitting and listening attentively, the jurors were getting restless, and no one objected when the Court adjourned for the morning break. Besides, by that time the court-reporter's fingers were probably smoking.

It wasn't going to be easy for Vogel to discredit Dr. Penrod. His testimony about the stages of human memory and how they may have affected Penny Beerntsen's identification of the defendant had been convincing. So rather than attacking the message, the prosecutor attacked the messenger instead.

This is the Midwest, and like every other region of the country, it has its own peculiar set of biases and prejudices. And Denis Vogel wasn't above taking advantage of them at trial. He made sure the jury understood exactly what kind of person Dr. Penrod was. Not only was he one of those high-powered expert witnesses for the defense, he was also an attorney, a psychologist, and a PhD from Harvard for crying out loud! What could he possibly know about the real world?

Not that Vogel was above bending a little psychology his way if it assisted the prosecution's theory of the case:

"Is there a term called 'feedback factor,' Mr. Penrod, do you know what that means?" Vogel asked confidently.

"I'm not sure what you're referring to," Penrod replied.

"Alright, when witnesses have a chance to get together and talk to each other about what they've seen, is there a psychological term for that?"

"Well, people may have coined a psychological term, but it's not one that's in widespread use."

"Have you done research in that area?"

"No, sir."

Vogel had reached a dead end, but it didn't matter – he made his point just by asking the question. He knew that Jim

Bolgert would be calling close to a dozen witnesses to back up Steve's alibi, and by asking Dr. Penrod about "feedback factor," he laid a foundation that he could use later to suggest that Steve's witnesses were all lying – that they got together and matched up their stories. And he did it through the defense expert, no less.

But Jim Bolgert was confident that Dr. Penrod had diminished the reliability of Penny's identification of his client, at least to some extent, so he moved on to the second prong of his defense – the alibi.

* * *

To testify or not to testify, that is the question. Not quite as existentially weighty as the question posed by Shakespeare in *Hamlet*, but it's the most agonizing decision an accused and his attorney face during trial.

A defendant has an absolute constitutional right not to testify, and the judge instructs the jury not to hold it against him if he decides not to. That's the theory. But in practice, the jury wants to hear from the defendant. "If he's innocent," they figure, "what's he got to hide?"

Constitutional niceties aside, Steven Avery really didn't have a choice. He'd been identified as the perpetrator of a despicable crime committed against an incredibly sympathetic victim, and no matter how much the judge instructed the jury about the presumption of innocence, the burden of proof, and the right not to testify, he simply had to take the stand.

So Steve took the stand and gave the jury a full accounting of his day, beginning with the errands he ran with Lori that morning and ending with their return from Green Bay later that night. He told them about pouring concrete at the salvage yard and about taking a ride on his four-wheeler with his sister in the quarry. And then he finished by credibly professing his innocence. Dennis Vogel tried to rattle him on cross, but for the most part, Steve held firm and improved his chances for an acquittal.

Next, Jim Bolgert called his client's wife to firm up the alibi. Lori Avery told the jury about their entire day – running errands in town that morning, visiting relatives at Steve's parents' in the afternoon, driving to Green Bay in the evening, and then coming back home later that night. She was a convincing, credible witness, who gave specific times and didn't try to dress things up. She gave the jury the same time-line that she gave to the police in her written statement the day after Steve was arrested, and the jury's ears especially perked up when she identified the receipt from ShopKo that proved they were in Green Bay at 5:13 pm.

Anticipating Vogel's cross-examination, Bolgert asked her if she spoke with her husband before she wrote the statement.

"No," Lori answered, "I didn't hear from Steve until a week later, on August 7, when he was allowed to make his first phone call."

"Did Steven ever tell you what to put in your statements?" Bolgert asked.

"No, he didn't even know I wrote them up."

"Did anybody tell you what to put in your statements, Lori?" Bolgert pressed.

"No, they didn't. I was there by myself when I wrote them."

Then, he asked her about one of her husband's more unusual habits. Penny Beerntsen had noticed that the assailant was wearing white underwear, an observation that wouldn't be very significant in most cases since most men wear white underwear. But it was in this one.

"Does Steve wear clothes when he sleeps?" Bolgert began.

"No, he doesn't," Lori responded, "just socks sometimes, if his feet are cold."

"Was he wearing underwear when he was arrested?"

"No, he wasn't – he doesn't wear underwear."

"Does he own any underwear?"

"No, he doesn't."

After Lori Avery was finished testifying, Bolgert called one witness after another to hammer home the alibi. They each repeated the same refrain: *Steve couldn't have assaulted Penny Beerntsen – we saw him at the Salvage Yard that day*. Marvin Mott was only there between one-thirty and two, but he saw Steve. Rose Scherer was there too. She looked out the window when *Divorce Court* was almost over, and Steve was still outside – and so was the cement truck. Chuck Avery saw Steve take his sister Barb to the gravel pit "at three or three-thirty or so." Steve's brother-in-law saw Steve and Barb go into the gravel pit too, though he couldn't recall what time. Lloyd Scherer helped Steve and the other guys pour concrete that day, and he remembered seeing Steve and his family leave at about ten minutes to four.

Judy Blanke was an especially effective witness for the defense. She and her husband were close friends of the Averys, and that afternoon they went to the Salvage Yard to cash in some aluminum cans. They arrived at about quarter to three, Mrs. Blanke testified, and while she was helping her husband unload the aluminum cans from the trunk, she saw Steve and a couple other guys smoothing out the cement. She even stopped to talk with them for awhile before going into the house to join the ladies. She said Steve came in at the end of *Divorce Court*, and now that she thought about it, she remembered him playfully turning off the TV to get a rise out of them.

The jury seemed especially interested when Mrs. Blanke described what happened when she and her husband Bill got ready to leave. She and Bill were getting into their car when she looked over and saw Steve loading the kids into his Blazer. Bill had recently washed the car and he didn't want any dirt on it, so he let Steve pull out of the gravel driveway ahead of them and they waited for the dust to settle before pulling out, themselves.

That kind of detail is hard to make up, and Mrs. Blanke came off as an honest and credible witness for the defense.

* * *

Denis Vogel knew his case would go straight down the toilet if the jury believed that Steve was still at the Salvage Yard when *Divorce Court* ended at three-thirty. So he had to convince the jurors that the Averys were lying and that the cement truck driver, Don Cigler, was the accurate reporter of time. His method of operation was to ask each member of the Avery clan on cross-examination if they had discussed the case amongst themselves. Most people could handle that question by confidently responding that of course they had, *wouldn't you? – he's part of our family*. But the Avery's aren't most people, and Vogel knew that no matter how they answered he couldn't lose. If they admitted they discussed the case, he could act like that was unusual and imply that they were trying to get their stories straight. Or if they lied and claimed they'd never discussed the case, the jury wouldn't believe them and they'd suspect they were lying about everything else too. Either way, their credibility would be shot.

Vogel's cross-examination of Steve's mother, Delores Avery, was particularly aggressive. He took off the gloves after she foolishly denied discussing the case with her husband or with other family members:

"You mean you didn't talk to your husband about the time when all the women got together, you didn't discuss that with anybody?" Vogel asked.

"No," Mrs. Avery replied.

"You didn't get together and try to remember what time it was you got together at your house?" Vogel pressed.

"No, huh-uh, because I know we watched *Divorce Court*, us women and all, so…"

Vogel interrupted: "You didn't sit down and discuss what time it was when he may have left the house that day?"

"No."

"So you and Allan haven't talked about this case at all?"

"Huh-uh, no," Mrs. Avery said unconvincingly.

"You talked about what happened on the day of the 29th amongst yourselves to try to figure out where everybody was and what everybody did, right?" Vogel insisted.

"I told you exactly what I remember."

"I know that. I'm just asking you, you have talked about it with the other people, trying to figure out what happened that day?"

Mrs. Avery stammered: "No, not about, no, I haven't."

"You haven't stood around," Vogel said, "and I'm not talking about the last couple of days, I'm talking about before the last couple of days when you've been to court – you stood around talking with the other people that have been here to just try to figure out what happened on the 29th?"

Then Mrs. Avery rallied: "I don't have to figure out what happened on the 29th – I know what happened on the 29th."

But Vogel persisted: "Right, but you've asked other people if they remember what happened on the 29th."

"No, I haven't."

Vogel wasn't done: "I'm not accusing you that because of talking to people there was any harm – I don't want you to get that impression," he lied. "I'm just asking if you talked amongst your family members about what happened on the 29th, and you said before that there were some statements that you heard, and I'm just trying to find out from you what those statements might have been, or who might have made those statements. Do you understand?"

But Mrs. Avery held firm: "Oh, I don't remember nothin' like that."

"That's all," Vogel said, finally leaving the defendant's mother alone.

Delores Avery had gone toe to toe with the district attorney and she hadn't flinched, so Jim Bolgert kept his re-direct examination short:

"Has all your testimony today been the truth?" he asked.

"Yes, it has," Mrs. Avery answered.

"Thanks. That's all I have."

Steve's sister Barb was next. Vogel tried pinning her down along the same lines he used with Delores Avery, but this time he even suggested that her brother's attorney had coached her about what to say. Barb sounded defensive in a few of her responses, but for the most part she handled herself well – especially about being coached by Bolgert.

Vogel's accusation that he coached his witness was hard to stomach for someone with Jim Bolgert's integrity, so in his re-direct examination, Bolgert put that one to rest immediately:

"Did anyone tell you what to say Barb?" he asked.

"No."

"Did I?"

"You just told me to be honest and tell the truth."

"Ms. Avery, did you sit down and discuss where Steve was that day and where he might have been – what he was doing?"

"No – 'cause I already knew."

"Did someone tell you to say you went down in the pit with Steve and his jeep?"

"No."

While Steve's wife, his sister, and his mother held their own on the stand, many of the other defense witnesses didn't fare so well. Denis Vogel's insinuation that they were lying about not discussing the case ahead of time tripped them up. Of course they discussed Steve's case. What family wouldn't talk about criminal charges filed against one of their own – especially if the charges could land the person in prison, like the charges in this case could.

But why did they lie if they didn't have to? Maybe they thought it would look bad if they admitted they talked to each other, maybe they couldn't distinguish between discussing Steve's case and hatching a plan to get him off, or maybe they're just not very sophisticated. But whatever the reason, when the Averys tried embellishing the defense, they smothered it instead.

But all things considered, when Jim Bolgert rested his case, he felt pretty good about the prospects for an acquittal. He believed firmly in his client's innocence, and left nothing on the table in presenting his defense. He had treated Steve and his family with dignity and respect since the day he was appointed, which, given the severity of the charges and, to put it mildly, their colorful personalities, not every defense attorney would be capable of or inclined to do.

He had cautioned each of his witnesses to be impeccably honest when they testified. For one thing, they could be charged with perjury if they weren't. But also, no matter how inconsequential the question, if the jury sniffed even the hint of a lie in the answer, they would discard the entire defense and promptly convict.

ELEVEN

T HE EVIDENCE WAS IN. The lawyers had called forty-three witnesses and introduced sixty-two exhibits. Soon, Steven Avery's fate would rest where it belonged – in the hands of twelve of his peers.

Judge Hazlewood read the standard instructions before the jury retired for deliberations. Packed full of legal concepts, jury instructions have a reputation for being boring and burdensome, but my sense is that most jurors listen to them attentively and a few even find them enlightening. He emphasized the instructions that listed the "elements" of each charge that the prosecution must prove, and after covering various other legal principles, he finished up with the instruction concerning the burden of proof:

> Ladies and gentlemen, the defendant is not required to prove his innocence. The burden of establishing every fact necessary to constitute guilt is upon the State. Before you can return a verdict of guilty, the

evidence must satisfy you beyond a reasonable doubt that the defendant is guilty. If you can reconcile the evidence upon any reasonable hypothesis consistent with the defendant's innocence, you should do so and find him not guilty.

Now in reaching your verdict, examine the evidence with care and caution. Act with judgment, reason, and prudence. The term "reasonable doubt" means a doubt based upon reason and common sense. It is a doubt for which a reason can be given, arising from a fair and rational consideration of the evidence or lack of evidence. It means such a doubt as would cause a person of ordinary prudence to pause or hesitate when called upon to act in the most important affairs of life. A reasonable doubt is not a doubt which is based upon mere guesswork or speculation. A doubt which arises merely from sympathy or from fear to return a verdict of guilty is not a reasonable doubt. A reasonable doubt is not a doubt such as may be used to escape the responsibility of a decision. Now, while it is your duty to give the defendant the benefit of every reasonable doubt, you are not to search for doubt. Rather, you are to search for the truth.

The duties of counsel have been performed, and the great weight of reaching a verdict is to be thrown wholly upon you, the jurors, called to exercise this important duty. You are not to be swayed by fear, sympathy, passion, or prejudice. You are to act with judgment, reason, and prudence. I charge you now to exercise your duty faithfully.

There were other instructions too, and perhaps a few of the jurors lost their concentration, but most of them paid close attention since a man's fate rested in their hands.

I once heard from a speaker at a prosecutors' conference that jurors are in a constant state of tension – they don't want to send an innocent man to prison but they don't want to set a guilty one free. The prosecutor's job, said the speaker, is to "ease their pain" by presenting the case so clearly and forcefully that the defendant's guilt is unmistakable.

It's great advice for clear-cut cases, but what if it's a case like this one, where the evidence is not so overwhelming? The law doesn't say the jury *can* find the defendant not guilty if they have a reasonable doubt – it says they *must*. But do jurors really give defendants the benefit of the doubt – especially when the crime is as vicious as this one and the victim as sympathetic as Penny Beerntsen? Steven Avery was about to find out.

* * *

The jury started deliberating right after dinner, but a few hours later they asked to see one of the exhibits. The police had confiscated Avery's shoes when they arrested him, and now the jury wanted to check them – probably for dried cement or particles of sand. After consulting with the lawyers, Judge Hazlewood sent the not-so-sweet smelling shoes of the defendant into the jury room.

The shoes contained neither cement nor sand, so the inspection didn't take long, and five minutes later – it was after midnight now – the jury made another request. This time, they wanted to see Exhibit No. 41.

Vogel and Bolgert exchanged glances as they watched the Clerk check the exhibit list and wondered what the hell Exhibit No. 41 was. The clerk turned the page, and there it was

– it was the note that Donald Cigler, the cement truck driver, had kept at home to keep track of his hours. Vogel had moved it into evidence on the second day of trial.

The lawyers knew it all along, and now the jurors' request for Cigler's notes confirmed it. When all the testimony was in and the exhibits admitted, when all the objections and arguments were over and the jury finally had the case, rubber would meet the road on one question. Close your eyes and you can almost hear Johnny Cochran making the argument: did the defendant have the TIME to commit the CRIME? Because if it doesn't fit… If Cigler's time-line was correct, he could have; if not, it was impossible – or at least close enough to impossible to create a reasonable doubt.

Jim Bolgert anxiously awaited the jury's decision in the dimly lit abandoned halls of the Manitowoc County Courthouse that night. Not only did he believe his client was innocent, but he also believed the jury would find him not guilty – the alibi was that strong. But they were taking an awfully long time, and he was becoming increasingly worried.

Was subconscious, or maybe not-so-subconscious, class bias playing a role in the deliberations? Bolgert hoped not, but when you put the Averys next to the Beerntsens … well, you get the point. What if some of the jurors didn't really care if the prosecution met its burden of proof? *He's probably assaulted other women*, they might be thinking, *and he probably assaulted Ms. Beerntsen, too*. Besides, why would the police arrest him if he wasn't the assailant, and why would the prosecutor be so certain he was guilty?

The jury retired at 1:45 a.m. without reaching a verdict, and deliberations resumed at nine the next morning. Six hours later, they finally reached a verdict.

The winter sun was already low in the sky when the jailers walked Steven Avery across the courtyard to receive his verdict. The lawyers feigned calm and put their game faces on as the jurors solemnly filed into the courtroom with their heads bowed down. Steve had been sweating it out over at the jail since ten o'clock the night before, and now he was about to learn his fate from twelve strangers that barely knew his name.

Judge Hazlewood addressed the foreman: "Mr. L. (*the author has omitted the jury foreperson's name*), I see you're holding some documents in your hands," he said calmly, "Has the jury reached a verdict?"

"Yes, Your Honor."

The courtroom was silent as Judge Hazlewood leafed through the verdict forms. Then he finally announced the verdict:

"Let the record reflect – I'm not going to drag this out – the verdict of the jury with regard to the charge of first degree sexual assault: 'Guilty'. With regard to the charge of false imprisonment: 'Guilty'. With regard to the charge of attempted murder in the first degree: 'Guilty'."

It was a clean sweep for the prosecution.

* * *

It's not unusual for a recently convicted offender to send a letter to the judge who presided over his trial. Maybe they're asking for a shorter sentence, maybe they're complaining about their lawyer, or the food in the jail. But rarely are they actually protesting their innocence. Steven Avery was one of the exceptions. On January 29, 1986, a month and a half after the jury had reached its verdict, he sent the following letter to Judge Hazlewood:

> Dear Judge Hazlewood,
> I am writing in regards to my case. I truly believe I did not get a fair trial. Why on god's green earth

would I go out and hurt a woman I don't even know and when I am Happily married and my wife just got out of the Hospital with our twins the day before. Why should My Wife have to raise our children alone, and Why should my kids have to grow up with out a father, especially When I did not do this and I am an innocent man.

I pray every night to god that the guy who did this Would turn himself in as I don't have a life setting up here and I have to worry about my Wife and 5 kids out there alone With that guy Still running around out there.

I really feel sorry of Mrs. Beerntsen as I Would not want anyone to have to go through something like that.

I know I have done some bad things in my past, but I started to realize it after I pulled an empty gun on Sandy Murphy that I Went about it in the Wrong Way and I started to turn my life around. I had heard that Sandy Murphy wanted to drop the charges against me but Mr. Vogel won't. Why is everybody against me, am I really that bad?

I was Wondering if you could please help me and my family as our future is in your hands.

I am scared shitless as to the outcome of my case and I am also scared for my family. I am not lieing with god as my Wittness. Please help me in any way you can I would Really appreciate it.

Thank you for your time.
please help me
thank you Judge

sincerely,
Steven Avery

On March 10, 1986, Judge Hazlewood sentenced Steven Avery to thirty-two years in the Wisconsin State Prison System – fifteen years for attempted first degree murder, fifteen years for first degree sexual assault, and two years for false imprisonment. The State owned Steve now. And since he was in the legal custody of the Department of Health and Social Services, they even changed his name – from now on, he was Inmate No. 018375.

Allan Avery called Judge Hazlewood on the morning after his son was sentenced. With a liberal sprinkling of garden-variety vulgarities along with a few more creative strings of expletives with repeated insertions of the "F" word, Mr. Avery insisted that Steve was innocent and his conviction was a travesty of justice. In a not so veiled threat, he asked Judge Hazlewood to release his .30-06 rifle because, in his words, he wanted "to start making his own probable cause determinations."

Here is the Judge's admirably patient and reasoned reply:

Dear Mr. Avery,

Your phone call to me on Tuesday, the 11th of March, 1986, requesting that I authorize the release of a 30-06 rifle to you is denied. My reasons are as follows:

1) The rifle is evidence in the pending case;
2) Your request – a phone call to my house at 7:30 AM in the morning, is not in proper form;
3) Your stated reason for requesting the gun back; that is, that you wanted to start making your own

probable cause determinations, is hardly a reason to give anybody a gun; and

4) I don't even know whether you own the gun or have any rightful claim to own it.

For the above reasons, your request for their return of the firearm is respectfully denied.

Very truly yours,

Fred H. Hazelwood, Circuit Judge.

Dodge Correctional Institution is located seventy miles southwest of Manitowoc in Waupun, and although it's one step below the State's "super-max" prison in Boscobel, it's impossible to get out of Dodge. Steven Avery was escorted through three sets of steel gates, and as he walked further and further into the labyrinth, each door clanged shut with a bang. It would be eighteen years before he'd walk out again, but unlike his anonymous arrival, his departure would be anything but tame.

PART II

TWELVE

W ISCONSIN HAS a two-tiered appellate court system. There's the Court of Appeals – and then there's the Supremes. Over ninety percent of all appeals start and finish in the Court of Appeals, so if you lose there, chances are good you've come to the end of the line and you might as well take your ball and go home. The Supreme Court can accept cases under three different scenarios: if the issue at hand is of statewide importance; if a decision is needed to clarify conflicting decisions among the lower courts; or if the interest of justice demands it. As to the third category, every appellant believes their case cries out for justice, but whether "the interest of justice" demands a review is in the eye of the beholder. The reality is that for the most part the Supremes leave the heavy lifting to the Court of Appeals, and that's what they did with the Avery case.

Appellate courts are reluctant to reverse a jury's verdict, or even to negate it and grant a new trial – otherwise, what's the point of having a jury decide? So it's not surprising that the majority of appellate court decisions are the same as those made by an NFL referee: "After further review, the play stands." Perhaps it's because they're so delusional about the rightness of their cause and can't imagine a higher court won't see it the same way they do, but given the small percentage of cases reversed by the Court of Appeals, offenders who feel they got a raw deal by the trial court are surprisingly confident about their chances on appeal.

In June 1986, three months after Steven Avery was sentenced, the State Public Defender's Office in Madison appointed Jack Schairer to represent him on appeal. Schairer reviewed the entire file and interviewed his client in prison, and the more time he spent on the case, the more convinced he became his client was innocent. This one was an easy call – he'd file an appeal.

But before he could even get to the Court of Appeals, the law required him to exhaust his remedies at the trial court level by filing a "Motion for Post-Conviction Relief." So on July 25, 1986, after just six weeks on the case, Jack Schairer filed his motion and requested Judge Hazlewood to grant his client a new trial "in the interest of justice."

He claimed he'd uncovered specific and material exculpatory evidence – that is, evidence that tended to negate the guilt of the accused. He also claimed the DA knew about the evidence and that his failure to disclose it robbed his client of a fair trial and his right to due process under the law. In the interest of justice, Schairer pleaded, his client deserved a new trial.

He also filed two other motions. One was a motion for bail pending appeal and the other was a motion for an *in camera* inspection of the prosecutor's file. He wanted Judge Hazlewood to review the prosecutor's file to determine if any other exculpatory evidence was withheld.

Denis Vogel fired back with a sworn affidavit, attesting that he'd faithfully complied with the discovery statute and had turned over to trial counsel a complete set of the police reports and everything else the defendant was entitled to. But then, with another high-profile conviction under his belt and a promising career ahead of him, Denis Vogel inexplicably resigned. He'd apparently landed a more lucrative position in a private law firm in Madison, so he and his wife shook the dust off their feet and promptly left town. The Governor tapped assistant district attorney Elma Anderson to fill the vacancy, but citing insufficient staff, Anderson appointed local attorney Ron Kaminski as a special prosecutor to handle the post-conviction motions in the Avery case.

Kaminski would describe years later how Tom Beerntsen appeared in his office almost daily to make sure he was up to speed. The last thing Tom wanted was for Penny to go through a second trial and have to re-live the assault all over again. But he need not have worried. Although Kaminski did mention to someone in the DA's office that he thought the case was weak, he was on top of the case and the State prevailed.

On September 29, 1986, Judge Hazlewood denied the defendant's motion for a new trial. In a written decision, he ruled that "none of the evidence characterized by the defense as exculpatory, either individually or collectively, materially affected the question of whether the defendant committed the assault."

The Judge also declined Jack Schairer's invitation to go fishing in the DA's file for other suspected exculpatory evidence, and he didn't even see the need for a formal hearing to consider the invitation: "At this point, there is no reason to believe that testimony will produce anything other than what has already been demonstrated by way of the affidavits on file," the Judge wrote. "The only interest of the defense that might be served by taking additional testimony would be to have an additional crack at the prosecution witnesses."

If Steven Avery was to be granted a new trial, it wouldn't be ordered by Judge Hazlewood – at least not on the basis of what was presented to him so far.

* * *

Having exhausted his remedies at the trial court level, Jack Schairer filed a Notice of Appeal with the Court of Appeals. Once again, he argued for a re-trial on the grounds that the DA had failed to disclose exculpatory evidence. But this time, he had to rely on his writing skills because oral argument is rare in the Court of Appeals – to be vocal, you must make it to the Supremes.

Schairer's brief was forty-nine pages long – and that didn't even include the appendix. What was this exculpatory evidence that Vogel supposedly withheld, anyhow?

It turns out the police interviewed a few other people who were out on the beach that day. Kathy Sang and her boyfriend were sailing a small sailboat a couple hundred yards from shore not far from where Penny Beerntsen was attacked. They kept close to the shoreline and occasionally swam back to the shore. Sang told an investigator from the State Public Defender's Office that she came across a woman jogging along the beach in a bikini at about three-thirty that afternoon. The woman turned around near a small creek that flowed into the lake and then headed back in the direction she came from. Sang said she had seen a man wearing a black shirt and long pants walking along the beach less than a half hour earlier. She said the man had a beer belly and his shirt was open in front with the shirt-tails exposed. The investigator showed her a photograph of Steven Avery, and she was sure of it – Avery was not the man she saw on the beach that day. She said she was interviewed by the police on the day of the assault and she believed she gave them a description of the man she saw on the beach.

Jack Schairer noted in his brief that defense counsel at the time, Reesa Evans-Marcinczyk, had filed a Supplemental Discovery Demand shortly after Avery was charged that specifically requested the State to produce "any and all evidence in its possession which would tend to show that a person other than the defendant committed the crime charged." Schairer had carefully reviewed everything in the file, and the police reports didn't mention anything about the man Kathy Sang saw on the beach that day.

It was clear that a short time before the assault a suspect other than Steven Avery was on the beach close to where Penny Beerntsen was attacked, and the State didn't inform the defense. Kathy Sang's description of the man she saw on the beach that afternoon was evidence the defendant was entitled to know, Schairer argued, and justice demands that he be granted a new trial.

He bolstered his argument by noting that the State's case hinged almost entirely upon the victim's identification of the defendant. Under these circumstances, he argued, evidence that shortly before the assault, a witness saw a suspicious man who didn't match the defendant's description might very well have led to an acquittal, especially because the defense had presented powerful evidence that Avery was somewhere else at the time of the assault.

Schairer's next line of attack concerned what police call a neighborhood canvass. In the days immediately following the assault, deputies from the Sheriff's Department conducted an extensive canvass in the neighborhood adjacent to Neshotah Park. They went door to door with one photograph of Steven Avery and another of his Chevy Blazer and asked if anyone saw the man or the vehicle depicted in the photos on the day of the assault. Nobody had.

The results of the neighborhood canvass, or even the fact that one was conducted, were not shared with the Defense. Schairer argued that given how close the case was, if the jury had known about the neighborhood canvass, they might have voted to acquit. In the interest of justice, he again demanded, the defendant should be granted a new trial.

His final argument concerned the observations of Steve's uncle, Deputy Arland Avery, on the night his nephew was arrested. Arland had noticed cement powder on Steve's shirt that night, but that fact wasn't disclosed to the Defense either. The presence of cement on the defendant's shirt would have significantly bolstered the alibi, Schairer argued, and had the jury known about it, his client might have been acquitted.

At the end of his forty-nine page brief, Schairer summed up his case for a new trial:

> While the State's evidence consisted primarily of the complaining witness' identification of the defendant as her assailant, the defendant called eighteen alibi witnesses and testified categorically denying any involvement in the crime. His alibi is consistent with the story he told the Sheriff at the station house right after he was arrested. However, the jurors were not told that Kathy Sang, the last person to have seen PB jogging before the assault, had seen another man on the beach near the time of the assault. Nor were the jurors told the police had conducted a canvas near the crime scene showing pictures of his vehicle to people in the area, and none of them identified him. Also, they did not know that Officer Avery had seen cement on Steve's clothing at the time of his arrest.

All of this evidence is exculpatory. And regardless of whether it's characterized as evidence improperly withheld by the State, newly discovered evidence, or evidence not presented due to the failure of defense counsel's investigation, this evidence warrants the granting of a new trial.

Assistant Attorney General Tom Becker was assigned to handle the appeal on behalf of the State, and on January 6, 1987, he wrote to the brand new Manitowoc County District Attorney, Jim Fitzgerald. Becker asked Fitzgerald to send him copies of any briefs or memorandums that his predecessor prepared in the trial court relating to the issues raised on appeal. Becker also sent a copy of Jack Schairer's brief for his review. Fitzgerald sent Becker a letter in reply indicating that he contacted former District Attorney Vogel, and Vogel told him that while he addressed some of the issues in the trial court, he hadn't prepared any formal briefs or memorandum.

So Becker filed his brief without any input from Vogel. He argued that the Defense hadn't proved the State withheld exculpatory evidence, so the conviction should stand. The Court of Appeals agreed, and on August 5, 1987, the Court issued its decision denying Avery's request for a new trial. Jack Schairer petitioned the Wisconsin Supreme Court to review the decision, but the Supremes promptly denied his Petition. Steven Avery had come to the end of the line.

* * *

At the same time Jack Schairer was seeking a new trial from the Court of Appeals, Steven Avery and his dad were seeking a pardon from the Governor. But in a heart-felt three page letter to Governor Tommy Thompson, Sandy Murphy, the reserve deputy's wife who Avery accosted at gunpoint back in

January of 1985, strenuously objected to the request. Murphy had read an article about Avery's pardon application in the local paper, and she wanted to weigh in with her opinion. If you're familiar with the politics of Tommy Thompson, then you know that Sandy Murphy had nothing to fear, but she was understandably concerned for her own safety and for that of the public in general if Avery was released, and she wanted to register her concerns.

She recounted the terror she felt when Avery pushed the muzzle of the gun into her face and told her to get into his car: "Avery never said what he planned to do to me," she wrote, "but after what he did to that woman on the beach that day, I can only guess. I hope in your wisdom you can see Mr. Avery for the kind of person he is," she continued, "and don't give him the chance to hurt anyone else. A person can only guess what Mr. Avery would be capable of doing if he's released."

* * *

On May 18, 1987, fourteen months after her husband was sentenced to prison, Lori Avery filed for divorce. Considering what Steve had put her through during their marriage, it's amazing she stayed with him as long as she did. With his wife filing for divorce, and with his plea for a new trial from the Court of Appeals and his petition for a pardon from the Governor both ending in failure, Steve channeled his energy into anger instead.

The letters started arriving soon after the divorce papers were filed. Lori wasn't overly concerned at first – Steve was bitter about the divorce, she figured, and pretty soon he'd get over it and move on. But the letters didn't stop. In fact, they continued for the entire time he was in prison, and they got worse and worse as time went on.

In early 1994, Steve started sending Lori sympathy cards:

"*May these words bring to you our most heartfelt sympathy*," was the message on one of them, to which Avery added in his own scratchy handwriting: "To my Love, Forever Lori – From Your Ex-husband Forever. Do You Love me? Tell me, then I will be good! And you can be my wife."

Another card read, "*With a love that is eternal, may your memories be the special bond that is forever shared with the one that you have loved*." On that one Steve scribbled, "Sorry for your mom and dad. From your Ex-husband. I don't want to be your Ex-husband at all – tell the kids I love them." A few weeks later he sent the same generic sympathy card and added, "I'm Sorry about your Daughter!" Love forever!

It was after Steve's next communication that Lori started getting scared. He'd sent an open records request to the Two Rivers Police Department a few months earlier seeking any current information he could get his hands on about Lori, including her address and any vehicles she owned. At first, the police department wisely denied the request, advising him that the open records law required specificity and pointing out that his request was too broad. But then Avery limited his request, and under the erroneous impression that Wisconsin's open records law required them to honor his request, the police department sent him the records. At least they made him pay the $1.57 copying fee up front.

A few weeks later, Lori received a diagram of her home with a note in Steve's handwriting indicating, "Home $19,000." There was also a picture of a minivan of the same make and model as hers with a notation that it was tan and it was "a piece of junk." He'd received the records concerning Lori's new address and her minivan from the police department, and he must have accessed the real estate and vehicle information from the computers in the prison that were provided for the inmates.

Lori scanned the torn note-book page and came across more of her ex-husband's chicken-scratch: "See yours Lori. Ha.-Ha – You don't knew what I'm going to do when I'm out, Do you? I do knew whats going to happen. It ant good at all? I Don't care if you hurt me. I Don't care!!!"

"I hate you, you got your divorce now you will pay for it," he wrote in an undated letter mailed to Lori from prison. In another letter, he wrote, "If you don't brang up my kids I will kill you. I promis. Ha. Ha."

Later, the letters got even worse. "Hi Lori ass," began one of them. "I hate you and your family!!! I hate you motherfuckers!! Hate, hate,You made me hate. I hate this Place!! You did this to me. I will be in trouble one more time when I get out and then I will die!!!!. Now I'm going to die when I get out so I don't care!"

Lori applied for a restraining order. It didn't matter that Steve was locked up in prison. Who's to say he couldn't contact someone on the outside to rough her up, or even worse – take one of the kids. Lori occasionally felt bad about what she still considered to be her husband's wrongful conviction, but it didn't matter anymore. Prison had turned him into a monster, and she was scared out of her mind.

THIRTEEN

IT'S TRUE – BLOOD really is thicker than water. So while Lori Avery understandably moved on with her life, Allan and Delores Avery continued to fight for their son's release. They would never give up on Steve. They were sure he was innocent, and they were determined to convince the justice system to set him free.

But Allan Avery knew the burden of proof had shifted, that no court would buy his son's claim of innocence unless he, himself, proved it beyond a reasonable doubt. So in late 1992 he hired a private investigator by the name of James Stefanic to see what he could dig up. Stefanic got a hold of the police reports from Jack Schairer and spent the better part of a week reviewing the file. Then he started snooping around.

First he interviewed Frank Butler, the local private investigator who worked with Schairer on Avery's first appeal. Butler told Stefanic he always felt there was something that just wasn't right with the Avery case. One of the officers saw cement dust on Steve's clothes when he was arrested, for example, but he was told he'd lose his job if he signed an affidavit saying so. Also, since Steve was denied visitors and phone privileges until eight days after he was arrested, it would have been impossible for the defense witnesses to make up the alibi. Butler said he didn't know whether it had anything to do with how the case was handled, but the victim and her husband were prominent members of the community, and the Sheriff knew them somehow. Also, during the five years he worked in Manitowoc, he never saw Sheriff Kocourek personally investigate another case – not once. "There's something people know they aren't saying," Butler explained. He was all set to interview Don Belz, the Captain at the Sheriff's Department who Allan Avery called the morning after his son's arrest, but then the door was shut and Belz wouldn't talk.

So Stefanic called Captain Belz, himself. Belz said he told Allan Avery he knew his son was innocent, but he couldn't do anything about it because the Sheriff told him not to talk about the case. "Between you and I," Belz, "there's a damn good possibility he's innocent."

Then he interviewed Arland Avery, Steve's uncle. Arland said Steve got "a railroad job." He told Stefanic the reason he helped arrest Steve that night was because he didn't want the SWAT team storming the house. He also said he saw cement powder on Steve's shirt and told Denis Vogel about it, but Vogel never asked him about it while he was on the witness stand. Stefanic noted in his report that "the cop who saw cement dust on Steve at the time of his arrest was told that if he signed an affidavit saying so, he'd lose his job."

Arland didn't have much good to say about the officers who interviewed Penny at the hospital that night either. He said Judy Dvorak was a reserve officer at the time and she'd do anything to get on the department full time. As for Gene Kusche's composite drawing, Arland said he thought Judy

Dvorak described Steve to Kusche before he even started the drawing.

Private investigator Stefanic also spoke with retired Detective Leo Jadowski. Leo said he never thought Avery was guilty. He wanted to reopen the case, but the Sheriff stood in the way.

He also interviewed Lori Avery. Lori told him the Sheriff's Department never liked Steve because he was always in trouble. "It was a vendetta," she said, "Steve fit the description, and they hung him – he was convicted before he went to Court." Lori said there was no way Steve could have committed the assault because he was with her the entire day.

Like every other investigator and attorney who worked on the case, Stefanic quickly became convinced that Steven Avery was innocent. But that wasn't enough to free him. For that, he'd have to find the guy who did it – he'd have to do some more digging.

He came up with three suspects as the fruits of his snooping, two from Sheboygan and one from Manitowoc. Then he called a detective friend at the Sheboygan County Sheriff's Department and asked him to check if any of them were on file, and if they were, could he run a check on them to see if any of them matched the victim's identification of the assailant. He explained that Avery wasn't even close to matching Penny Beerntsen's initial description of the assailant. She said he was 5'6" to 5'7", with long sandy hair, a brown scraggly beard, and brown eyes. But Avery's only five feet tall – 5'1" at most, and he has blue eyes, not brown. She also said the assailant was in his early thirties, but Avery was only twenty-three at the time of the assault.

The detective from Sheboygan came up empty – none of the three names fit the description. But Stefanic didn't give up. On May 22, 1993, he sent a letter to WBAY-TV in Green

Bay outlining the case for Steve's innocence. He included the relevant documents to prove it and concluded with, "I believe that an innocent man is in prison for a crime he did not commit." WBAY never followed up.

FOURTEEN

THE SCIENCE OF deoxyribonucleic acid, DNA, was just beginning to seep into the practice of law in the early 1990s. The nation's top-notch criminal defense attorneys immediately grasped its potential. They saw in DNA a great new hope for wrongfully convicted defendants who had exhausted their remedies for relief in the courts of appeal. With increasingly sophisticated methods of analysis to identify its genetic footprints, DNA gave them one more shot to prove their clients' innocence.

Attorney Steven Glynn of Milwaukee is one of those top-notch attorneys. He's widely regarded as one of the best, if not the best, criminal defense attorney in the state of Wisconsin. As a lawyer friend of mine once put it, Steve Glynn has the whole package – he's an expert in the law, but he's also great with a jury. His intelligent appearance and gentleman's demeanor make you like him immediately – and his full mane of once premature gray hair effect a reassuring wisdom.

Sales of junk cars must have been brisk in the mid-1990s because in October 1994, seven years after the Court of Appeals rejected the defendant's first appeal, Allan Avery retained Steve Glynn to represent his son. Like the attorneys before him, Glynn and his associate, Robert Henak, reviewed the entire file – the police reports, the crime lab reports, transcripts from the motion hearings and from the trial, and other miscellaneous papers common to a lawyer's file. They had their work cut out for them – the trial transcript alone was 1,029 pages long.

The lawyers were on the lookout for evidence that might contain DNA. The police had retrieved a good deal of physical evidence – hair, blood, clothing, fingernail scrapings – from both the defendant and the victim and Glynn hoped it was still around. He sent a letter to District Attorney Fitzgerald, advising him that he'd been retained to investigate and pursue post-conviction relief on behalf of Steven Avery. He asked Fitzgerald if the physical evidence still existed, and if it did, to make sure it wasn't destroyed.

Jim Fitzgerald had defeated Elma Anderson in a hotly contested race for District Attorney back in 1986. Both he and Elma were assistant district attorneys under Denis Vogel, and although Elma was appointed by the Governor after Vogel unexpectedly left town, she had to run in an election six months later. Fitzgerald threw his hat in the ring, and after the recently-departed but still well-connected Denis Vogel threw his political weight behind him, he defeated Anderson and became the new DA.

Now it was eight years later and Fitzgerald had inherited the Avery file. He called the Sheriff's Department after he received Glynn's letter, and asked if they still had the physical evidence from the Avery file. None other than Chief Inspector Gene Kusche replied a few days later by memo.

Gene said he checked the evidence room at the Sheriff's Department, and there was no physical evidence from the Avery case on file.

Fitzgerald thought he better check with the Clerk of Courts' Office – maybe the court file would at least have the physical evidence that was introduced during the trial. A week or so later, the chief deputy clerk – there's never a shortage of chief deputies in government – advised Fitzgerald by memo that she finally had a chance to look for the exhibits. She found them in a box that was stored in the communal vault in the Courthouse basement. She explained that she hadn't taken the exhibits out of the box, but it looked like they were all there. She also noted in her memo that Gene Kusche had stopped in a few weeks earlier looking for the evidence.

Fitzgerald called Steve Glynn to tell him the evidence had been preserved in the court file, and they arranged a time for Glynn to come up to Manitowoc to view the exhibits. Glynn drove up a few days later and pored over the contents of the box. Two of the exhibits immediately caught his eye. The first was a loose pubic hair, possibly the assailant's, that was collected from the victim on the night of the assault. The second was biological material that was retrieved from scraping underneath the victim's fingernails. Either one could contain the biological blueprint of the true assailant and prove Steven Avery's innocence once and for all.

One more thing about the box. That same box would be retrieved from the basement vault again in connection with another court proceeding ten years later, and Avery's lawyers would raise Cain about lax security procedures for storing evidence in the Clerk of Courts Office.

* * *

A few weeks later, Steve Glynn filed a post-conviction motion in the trial court seeking release of the pubic hair and the fingernail scrapings for DNA analysis. Still on the bench, Judge Hazlewood conducted the hearing a few months later. Glynn asked the Court to release the evidence so it could be tested for DNA and run through the State's new sex offender DNA data bank. The case was an extremely close one, he argued, and since the day he was arrested, his client has consistently professed his innocence.

Under the law, newly discovered evidence is not a sufficient basis for granting a defendant a new trial unless the evidence creates a reasonable probability that there would be a different result on retrial. At first blush, the pubic hair and the fingernail scrapings from the Court file weren't "new evidence" since they existed at the time of the original trial. But Glynn argued that they should be treated as such because current DNA analysis employs science that did not exist back then, so depending upon the results of the testing, his client should be granted a new trial. All he's asking, he pressed convincingly, is to have it re-tested. And besides, wouldn't the public itself benefit if the test results proved his client was innocent – especially if there was a hit in the data bank and the real assailant was brought to justice?

Jim Fitzgerald argued that Glynn hadn't laid a sufficient foundation to justify re-testing the evidence. But Judge Hazlewood sided with defense and granted the motion: "It's arguably probable that the result of the testing may be beneficial and consistent with justice," he ruled, "and justice is best served by allowing a test under controlled conditions by agencies, persons, or entities with appropriate skills in this area."

The attorneys settled on a private firm in Virginia – Laboratory Corporation of America – to conduct the DNA analysis. It took a long time, but nine months later, the results were finally in.

The scientist who performed the analysis, Anita Lynn Matthews, compared the DNA in the pubic hair and the fingernail scrapings to known samples of DNA from Penny Beerntsen and Steven Avery. The pubic hair did not contain a sufficient amount of biological material for analysis, but the fingernail scrapings did. A portion of the specimen contained Penny Beerntsen's DNA, but both Penny and Avery were excluded as possible contributors to the rest. The bottom line – someone else's DNA was retrieved from underneath Penny's fingernails after the assault.

Armed with physical evidence suggesting someone other than Steven Avery committed the assault, Glynn called Judge Hazlewood's judicial assistant and scheduled a hearing on his motion. The defense would be requesting a new trial based upon newly discovered evidence under Wisconsin Statutes Section 974.06.

A few weeks later, Glynn filed a second unrelated motion. Like Jack Schairer did in Avery's first appeal ten years earlier, he alleged that the State had withheld exculpatory information. But this time, it wasn't about a mystery man on the beach or a neighborhood canvass that came up empty. This time, the allegation was more specific and it sounded like it might even have teeth.

Never accused of being overly discreet, former Detective Leo Jadowski had spilled the beans. Leo told Glynn's investigator that the Sheriff's Department had identified an alternate suspect from Sheboygan County early on in the investigation, who matched the description of the assailant, but the prosecution never shared the information with the defense. Glynn argued that the State's conduct violated his client's right to due process under the law and entitled him to a

131

new trial. He also wanted to ferret out the facts at an evidentiary hearing.

Jim Fitzgerald got right on it. He instructed the newly promoted Chief Inspector Gene Kusche to interview each of the detectives who worked the case back in 1985 and ask them if they ever heard about an alternative suspect from Sheboygan. Over the next several weeks, Kusche conducted a series of interviews, and although several of the detectives had retired, he managed to catch up with all of them. The settings for the interviews varied: some were at retired detectives' residences, one was at a restaurant, and another was at Leo Jadowski's pawn shop.

Kusche tape recorded each of the interviews and then forwarded the transcripts to Fitzgerald so he could prepare for the hearing. The detectives circled the wagons: *Who, me? I never heard anything about an alternative suspect*, was the common refrain. Years later, though, an independent investigation conducted by the Wisconsin Department of Justice would suggest otherwise.

* * *

On July 30, 1996, Judge Hazlewood conducted the hearing on Steve Glynn's motion for a new trial. Anita Lynn Matthews, the scientist from the lab in Virginia who tested the fingernails and the hair, testified by phone.

She started out by explaining the fundamentals of DNA science and the latest testing procedures. DNA stands for deoxyribonucleic acid, she explained. It's a microscopic chemical compound found in the nucleus of every cell in our bodies. It's divided into pairs of spiraled strands – double helixes they call them. Each cell contains about ten thousand double helixes, and each double helix contains twenty-three pairs of chromosomes, with one member of each pair coming from the mother and one from the father.

"As human beings," Matthews continued, "we share many physical traits – we all have hair and eyes and skin, for example, so we have many similarities in our DNA. But there are regions on each strand of our DNA called loci, where the number and the order of chromosomes vary from one person to another. It's these regions that scientists examine to identify the source of a particular specimen of DNA."

Then Glynn asked her how scientists test the DNA to determine who it came from. Matthews explained:

"Police submit a questioned sample, or specimen, of biological material – blood, skin, hair, semen, saliva, that sort of thing, along with a known sample that was collected from the suspect. DNA testing is simply a comparison of the DNA patterns between the questioned sample and the known sample. If the DNA profiles are consistent with each other, then they could have originated from the same source, and we assign a statistical likelihood of that, such as 1 in 2 billion Caucasians, or 1 in 5 billion Hispanics, etcetera. On the other hand, if the DNA profiles are different from each other, then they could not have originated from the same source."

"What did you find in this case?" Glynn asked.

"In this case, there were two questioned samples – fingernail scrapings and a pubic hair – and the two known samples, one purported to be from Penny Beerntsen and the other from Steven Avery."

"Specifically, how did you analyze the pubic hair and the fingernail scrapings in this case," Glynn asked.

"The DNA testing performed in this case involved first purifying the DNA in one-half of the evidentiary sample to remove cellular debris, resulting in a clean DNA solution. Then I used the polymerase chain reaction (PCR) technique to amplify the DNA at the specific regions, or loci, where variability is generally noted. PCR essentially copies the DNA until there is enough to analyze. Then a detection method is applied to visualize the different 'alleles,' or forms of DNA, which are present at each locus, permitting a comparison of the DNA in the evidentiary sample with that from the known samples."

Matthews explained that after isolating DNA from the preparations of the fingernail-scrapings, she was able to characterize the DNA at three loci. The results of the first sample were consistent with the known sample of DNA from Penny Beerntsen. But the results of the second sample indicated a mixture of DNA from at least two individuals. And, as Matthews testified, "neither Penny Beerntsen nor Steven Avery could have contributed to the number eight allele – it had to have come from some person other than Steven Avery or Penny Beerntsen."

Jim Fitzgerald fought tooth and nail against the defendant's request for a new trial. The defendant's own expert can't say who else contributed to the DNA, he argued, only that it doesn't belong to either the defendant or to the victim. And he reminded the Court that Matthews admitted on cross-examination that DNA can be transferred casually. It could have come from the victim's spouse, her children, or even the nurse who collected the fingernail scrapings at the hospital that night – Lord only knows.

"The only new evidence the defendant really has," Fitzgerald said, "is that some of the DNA underneath the victim's fingernails came from somebody else, Judge, and that's not enough for this Court to grant a new trial."

Judge Hazlewood agreed with Fitzgerald, and on September 23, 1996, he issued a written decision denying both the defendant's motions. He agreed with Glynn that the DNA evidence was "truly newly discovered in the sense that the type of DNA testing at issue here didn't exist in a practical sense at the time of the trial." But in order to warrant a new trial, the Judge explained, the newly discovered evidence must create a reasonable probability that there would be a different result on retrial, and in this instance, he ruled, it didn't. Motion denied!

The ruling on Glynn's second motion – that the prosecution failed to disclose information about an alternate suspect from Sheboygan – was even worse for the defense. Fitzgerald had planned to call each of the detectives and former-detectives that Kusche had interviewed, but Judge Hazlewood denied the Motion without even granting the defendant a hearing, so the detectives didn't even have to testify.

* * *

Steve Glynn did what every good defense attorney does who loses at the trial court level but still believes in the rightness of his client's cause – he appealed. So ten years after the conviction, and five years since the initial appeal, the case of *State of Wisconsin vs. Steven A. Avery* was back in District II of the Wisconsin Court of Appeals.

As Jack Schairer did in the first appeal, Glynn began his brief by pointing out that Penny Beerntsen was the sole eyewitness against his client and the only one to identify him. Sixteen other witnesses testified that Avery was elsewhere at the time of the attack, but the jury nonetheless convicted him.

Then he got to the meat of his argument:

"Given the extent of her injuries and the blood on her hands, one source of the DNA underneath the victim's fingernails was certainly the victim herself. Likewise, given her clawing at the assailant and his forcing her to stroke his penis with her right hand while grabbing that hand with his own, another source was almost as certainly the assailant. While the DNA results themselves could not show whether there were only two sources, the most likely conclusion on the facts in this record is that there were only two – the victim and her assailant."

He also addressed the State's argument that the DNA could have come from someone other than the perpetrator: "It was the perpetrator whom the victim clawed at with such force as to break her own fingernails, and it was the perpetrator who forced her to stroke his penis with her right hand. The State's assertion that the DNA could have originated from some sort of casual contact with someone else is wholly speculative on this record."

Then he addressed the trial court's denial of his second motion – the request for a new trial based upon the State's failure to disclose they had an alternative suspect in Sheboygan. He argued that Judge Hazlewood erred when he summarily denied the Motion without permitting him to call the detectives who investigated the case and question them on the record:

"Evidence that the Sheriff's Department had identified an alternate suspect in the next county who matched the description of the perpetrator is material and exculpatory," he began. "This was an extremely close case, and the withheld information goes directly to the sole contested issue at trial, that of identification. There was a strong case on Mr. Avery's side in terms of alibi, and no physical evidence tied him to the crime. Under these circumstances, evidence that someone else from a nearby county who resembled the assailant was suspected by the police creates a reasonable probability of a different result on retrial."

But on September 3, 1997, the Court of Appeals sided with the State and affirmed the lower court's decision. Glynn filed a Petition for Review with the Wisconsin Supreme Court a few weeks later, but the petition was promptly denied. For the second time in the eleven years since he was convicted, Steven Avery came up short in his quest for a new trial.

Steve Glynn was disappointed with the Court's decision, but he wasn't really surprised since he knows the cards are stacked heavily against defendants when their case goes up on appeal. Avery, on the other hand, was more than just disappointed – he was devastated. He'd spent the last eleven years of his life in prison for a crime he swore he didn't commit, years he should have spent on the outside with Lori and the kids and the rest of the Avery clan. Instead, he and Lori were divorced and he was estranged from his children. The State had taken it all away.

FIFTEEN

MY WIFE JODY and I moved to Manitowoc in the fall of 1991. I was a prosecutor in suburban Milwaukee, but a few years after we were married we wanted to move on. So we kept our eyes open for an assistant district attorney position in the central part of the state and before we knew it, two counties posted openings – one in Calumet County and the other in Manitowoc. I must have fooled the interviewers pretty well because both counties offered me the job, which was good news, but it also meant we had to choose. So we spent a weekend checking out our prospects.

Calumet County has its own kind of charm, but we fell in love with Manitowoc almost immediately. With a healthy respect for its past, Manitowoc rightly boasts of its shipbuilding heritage. The city is officially designated the Maritime Capitol of Wisconsin, though sixty miles to the north Sturgeon Bay still fights for the title. Visit the Wisconsin Maritime Museum and you can tour the *U.S.S. Cobia*, an authentic WW2 submarine that's docked in the river. Among other things, you'll learn that 28 of the 211 US subs built during WWII were built right here in Manitowoc. Sadly though, the city's shipbuilding industry has been in serious decline for decades. The largest and most storied of the old firms, the Manitowoc Company, no longer even builds ships here. All that remains is Burger Boat, founded in 1863, which sells one-hundred-fifty foot luxury yachts to Arab sheiks and NBA basketball players and with the recent jolt to the nation's economy, now even Burger Boat is struggling.

We walked along the main street in the historic and touristy downtown, and then we came upon the Courthouse at the intersection of Eighth and Washington. We looked up at the century old stately stone building capped off by a dome, and then we walked inside.

Listed on the prestigious National Register of Historic Places, the Manitowoc County Courthouse is just one of Wisconsin's many well-preserved historic county courthouses. When local citizens built it at the turn of the century – the one before the last turn that is – the city's shipbuilding industry was in its heyday and the county coffers must have been flush with dough. Using materials like dolomite limestone and Italian marble, construction began in 1902 and was completed four years later.

Classical architecture inspires the Manitowoc County Courthouse – its beauty comes from its integrity, its balance, its order. Indeed, Lady Justice herself couldn't have designed a more gorgeous courthouse than ours. On the outside, huge slabs of purple sandstone anchor the foundation, and the three-story symmetrical main structure gives way to a now oxidized copper abutment that supports a towering dome. The dome used to be made of glass, but now it consists of plain looking sheets of dulled gray steel. Solid pillars, six to a floor, support a gigantic atrium inside, where marble stairs worn smooth by a century of climbing litigants carry visitors from one floor to the next under the light of a massive chandelier hanging precisely half way down from the top of the dome. People who work there have grown accustomed to its beauty, but if you gaze up you'll see four murals, each depicting a classical image of justice, spaced across the curvature of the dome.

Manitowoc County Court House with its dome shrouded in fog off Lake Michigan

For fifty years, natural light filtered in through the glass panes of the dome during the day, and artificial light shined forth at night, displacing the darkness like light from a cathedral. Then on June 28, 1950, a terrific hailstorm swept through the city and obliterated the dome. The glass, of course, was fragile, like the lives of many who were caught up in the stress and uncertainty of the justice system inside, and when the storm struck it shattered the glass to pieces. Construction workers did their best to restore the dome by replacing the glass with steel, but eventually even steel corrodes, and after a few decades, the courthouse dome came to look unsightly.

* * *

But it wasn't the charm of the city or even the gorgeous county courthouse that inspired us to settle here. It was the beauty of nature. Driving north along Lake Michigan's shoreline between Manitowoc and Two Rivers, Jody gazed out the window while I snuck an occasional view from behind the wheel. The lake curves gracefully here, the vast, endless waters drawing you in. They say every lake has its own personality – Lake Michigan has several. Unruffled and undisturbed one day, it can be wildly impulsive and agitated the next. And like all lakes, it's mostly the weather that determines the Great Lake's demeanor. If it's a clear summer day on land, then the lake looks warm and inviting too, turning deep blue or at times even tropical green. But if the weather turns ugly, if the sky is gray and foreboding, then the lake turns ugly too, and you can barely discern the horizon.

But the lake was neither calm nor foreboding when Jody and I drove north toward Two Rivers that day. With fog hugging the shoreline, it was full of mystery instead. It's rare to see an iron ore ship from the western shore of Lake Michigan – they generally stick to the middle. But there it was, shrouded in fog, seemingly suspended above the surface of the water, a monstrous iron ore ship appeared out of nowhere – motionless and timeless in the choppy waters just a half mile out to sea. I learned later that the brisk northwesterly wind is why the giant ship was hugging the shore that day – it was seeking shelter from the wind-driven swells. Looking back, we both think it was partly the mystery and the romance of that ship that brought us here.

* * *

Becoming a lawyer wasn't something I aspired to when I grew up, so like a lot of attorneys, I went to law school by default. But something strange happened a few years after moving here: I came to enjoy my reluctantly chosen profession. Shy and reserved by nature, to be an effective prosecutor I found I couldn't be either. As a prosecutor, I had to take control of the tempo, hustle the ball up the court – you name the sports metaphor – but being shy and reserved wouldn't cut it for sure.

More, though, I was dealing with real people with real problems. Someone's got to do it, but fighting over which of two multi-billion dollar advertising companies infringed upon the other one's trademark, or schmoozing with well-heeled corporate clients while climbing over my peers, isn't my shtick, and I'd fall flat on my face if I tried. But guiding a devastated victim through the trauma of a jury trial, or encouraging a small time offender going through a rough stretch to turn his life around is something I could sink my teeth into, and as a bonus I could even try to do what I thought was right.

SIXTEEN

S TEVEN AVERY HAD already spent six years in prison by the time Jody and I moved to Manitowoc, and over the next several years the main players in the Avery saga moved on. Sheriff Kocourek retired after a distinguished career in public service, and Chief Inspector Kusche soon followed, but Steven Avery continued to rot in prison, not knowing where to turn.

But his parents persevered, and three years after the Court of Appeals rejected their son's second plea for a new trial they encouraged him to apply for legal assistance with the Wisconsin Innocence Project, one of several clinical programs at the University of Wisconsin's Law School in Madison. Under the direction of professors from the law school, a dozen or so students at the Innocence Project investigate claims filed by state prisoners who claim they were wrongfully convicted. Like similar programs throughout the country, much of the Wisconsin Innocence Project's work in recent years has focused on DNA.

143

When Steve Glynn handled Avery's second appeal in 1996, DNA science was still in its infancy and its forensic value was extremely limited. But advances in technology during the late nineties and the first years of the new century allowed scientists to examine smaller and smaller units of biological material for DNA, which was good news for wrongfully convicted defendants. The faculty and students at the Wisconsin Innocence Project hoped to use the new technology to uncover hard proof that Steve was innocent.

In the spring of 2001, two of those students contacted the District Attorney to see if he would stipulate to re-testing the physical evidence for DNA. Jim Fitzgerald was reluctant. He told the students his recollection was that there was physical evidence that directly tied Mr. Avery to the crime. He asked them to review the one thousand twenty-nine page trial transcript and then direct him to the portions that referred to physical evidence so that he could make a decision.

The students reviewed the transcript and then sent him the following letter:

Dear Mr. Fitzgerald,

We have reviewed the trial transcripts as you requested. Enclosed please find those parts of the State's case which address the issue of microscopic hair evidence.

The hair found "consistent" by Ms. Culhane was the only physical evidence tying Mr. Avery to the victim in this matter. Testimony by Ms. Culhane about that hair consisted of approximately twenty-five pages. Testimony by three other witnesses was offered solely for the purposes of establishing a chain of custody and/or emphasizing the importance of the 'consistency' testimony by Ms. Culhane.

Please let us know what else, if anything, we can provide for you.

The case languished for months without a response from Fitzgerald, and the law students eventually concluded he wasn't going to stipulate. So under the direction of Professor Keith Findley, one of the co-directors of the Innocence Project, they filed a motion for post-conviction DNA testing and scheduled it for a hearing in front of Judge Hazlewood.

On March 22, 2002, almost a year after the Innocence Project first contacted Jim Fitzgerald, Steven Avery was back in court for another motion hearing. Steve was in good spirits, grateful to be out of prison if only for a day and full of hope that he'd be given another chance to prove his innocence.

Keith Findley argued the case for the defense, and Fitzgerald objected on behalf of the State. At the end of the hearing, Judge Hazlewood said he wanted to take some time to review his notes – he'd make a decision from the bench in a few weeks. Twelve days later, with the defendant appearing by phone from prison this time, the Judge granted the motion. He asked the attorneys to see if they could reach a stipulation concerning which pieces of evidence should be tested for DNA and how to ensure their safekeeping during transport.

The parties filed a stipulation a few weeks later enumerating the items they agreed should be tested. Included in the list were thirteen hairs that were recovered from Penny Beerntsen on the night of the assault. Judge Hazlewood signed an Order directing the Clerk to seal the evidence and release it to a deputy sheriff for transport to the Crime Lab. The Order included a provision that if there was a sufficient DNA profile for comparison, the Crime Lab was to return any remaining evidence to the Clerk of Courts, where it would be preserved. If there wasn't a sufficient sample, the Crime Lab was to contact the Court and await further instructions.

But then there was a problem. The stickers identifying the exhibits had fallen off, presumably because the glue had dried. A month later, two students from the Innocence Project wrote to Steve to explain the hold-up. They were recently assigned to his case, so first they introduced themselves, and then they got to the point:

"We have spoken with the District Attorney regarding the evidence you would like re-tested," they wrote. "As you may know, the labels have fallen off the exhibits, and it has now become necessary to arrange a time with the DA to re-label the evidence. Hopefully, once the pertinent evidence has been identified, we will be able to get the DNA testing process underway shortly thereafter."

A fresh pair of law students was handling his case now, and after more than a year of trying to get some damned hairs retested, the evidence in the court file couldn't even be identified. Avery was tickled pink.

It took four more months to clear up the sticker problem, and it wasn't until September 16, 2002, six days after Jim Fitzgerald lost his bid for re-election, that he presented the Court with an amended Order to transport the evidence to the Crime Lab. Penny Beerntsen wasn't happy either. She had tried repeatedly to find out the status of the re-testing of the physical evidence, but Jim never returned her calls.

* * *

The scientists at the Wisconsin State Crime Lab analyze all manner of physical evidence – guns, drugs, fibers, fingerprints, blood, hair, semen, saliva, handwriting exemplars, and a whole lot more. Every day, police agencies and district attorneys across the state bombard the Crime Lab with requests to test physical evidence – especially for DNA.

But DNA analysis is painstaking work and it takes time. The result is an ever-growing backlog that has even become a hot button political issue in recent State Attorney General elections. Add that pending trial cases receive priority over cases on appeal, and it's not surprising that it took almost a year for the Crime Lab to analyze the re-submitted evidence in the Avery case for DNA.

But now the results were in. Eighteen years earlier, on a warm summer night in July 1985, a nurse at Memorial Hospital retrieved thirteen loose pubic hairs from Penny Beerntsen's body, any of which could have been left behind by the man who assaulted her. The nurse placed them in a "sex crimes kit" and handed the kit to Deputy Dvorak, who transported the evidence to the Crime Lab, where serologist Sherry Culhane examined the hairs, doing her level best with the science and technology available at the time.

Still working at the Crime Lab eighteen years later, now Culhane examined the hairs again – this time looking for DNA. She observed detectable amounts of DNA on only two of the thirteen hairs. She compared the DNA profiles of the two hairs with known samples of DNA from Penny Beerntsen and Steven Avery. The DNA from one of the hairs matched Penny Beerntsen. But the DNA from the final hair – and the final hope for Steven Avery – matched neither.

Culhane ran the DNA profile of the hair against the State and federal DNA databases and waited for the reply. She received a hit! The DNA profile on the final hair matched Wisconsin State Prison Inmate Number 167930, a convicted sex offender by the name of Gregory A. Allen, who was currently serving a sixty year prison sentence for a brutal rape that he committed ten years after he assaulted Penny Beerntsen.

Three highly skilled defense attorneys had spent enormous amounts of energy and untold hours to prove their client was innocent, but after eighteen years, their efforts proved impotent. In the end, what freed Steven Avery wasn't the law. What freed him was an infinitesimally small amount of a chemical compound inside the nucleus of the cells in one pubic hair that was recovered by a nurse on the night of the assault. Thank God for DNA.

SEVENTEEN

D ISTRICT ATTORNEY MARK Rohrer had been in office for less than six months when the Avery case exploded on the morning of September 3, 2003. Rohrer had succeeded Jim Fitzgerald by a circuitous route. In the summer of 2002, for what I thought then and still believe were legitimate reasons, I decided to run for DA. There hadn't been a contested election for the District Attorney in Manitowoc County since 1986, when Jim won a close election against Elma Anderson after the recently departed but still influential Denis Vogel threw him his support. Jody and I ran a positive but aggressive campaign, and with lots of help from family and friends, we won. But I'd worked myself to exhaustion, and when I began feeling symptoms similar to what I felt at the onset of a serious depression I'd struggled through years earlier, I decided not to take the office we'd fought so hard for. Governor Jim Doyle appointed my campaign manager, Mark Rohrer, to serve as the District

Attorney, and when the depression I had feared never materialized, I stayed on as an assistant DA.

In the short time Mark had been in office, we had already dealt with a couple of drunk-driving fatalities and a first degree intentional homicide. He was also feeling the stress from taking over an office that had been neglected for years. With all that on his plate, he needed help or sometimes just a good ear, and since I was a trusted friend and a prosecutor with fifteen years experience under my belt, I was often that ear.

On the morning of September 3, all three courtrooms were packed with plea dates, pretrial conferences, and preliminary examinations. As I was walking out of Branch 3, Mark hurriedly approached me and said something about the DNA test results being in on an eighteen year old sexual assault case. Could I join him in his office? The Crime Lab had called, and he still had the analyst on the phone.

So I walked into Mark's office, and Sherry Culhane was on speakerphone. Sherry said she was calling about the Steven Avery case. She'd completed the DNA analysis and suggested we have a seat before she told us the news. Then she told us. The DNA profile from one of the questioned hairs recovered from the victim matched a convicted sex offender serving time for a first degree sexual assault in Green Bay. His name was Gregory Allen. Sherry explained the statistical likelihood that it was not Allen's hair was 1 in 251 billion in the Caucasian population, 1 in 162 billion in the African American population, 1 in 1 trillion in the Southeast Hispanic population, and 1 in 49 trillion in the Southwest Hispanic population. Allen is Caucasian, and although Sherry didn't use the word "match", for all practical purposes, we could treat it as Gregory Allen's hair.

Mark and I looked at each other in disbelief – it's as if a bomb exploded. Neither of us had ever heard of Gregory Allen.

In fact, we knew very little about the Avery case itself, other than that it involved the brutal assault of a prominent local woman along the beach on Lake Michigan. Mark was still an undergraduate when Avery was convicted, and by the time Jody and I moved here, Avery had already spent six years in prison. Jim Fitzgerald hadn't relayed any of the issues or facts involved in the Avery case after the election, and he said nothing about a DNA analysis being done on a pubic hair that might soon prove consequential.

The Avery "file" consisted of hundreds of documents that were packed inside expandable file folders in three separate boxes, and the boxes were still in Jim's corner office, the office now occupied by Mark. I started skimming through the file while we were still on the phone. Starting with what looked like the most organized part of the file, I came across some police reports and an attached criminal complaint that didn't belong in the file. What caught my attention was the name of the defendant – Gregory Allen. It was the same name that Sherry Culhane just told us was the real assailant. *That's kind of strange*, I thought.

Then I skimmed the criminal complaint. On August 2, 1983 – almost two years to the day before Penny Beerntsen was attacked – Gregory Allen was charged with exposing himself and lunging at a woman who was walking her dog along the same beach where Penny was assaulted two summers later. I flipped to the signature line on the last page to see who prosecuted the case against Allen. It was Denis Vogel. "Holy shit," I said out loud.

Sherry Culhane had given Gregory Allen's identifying information to Mark so we could run a record check on CCAP – the Wisconsin Circuit Court's website. Mark still had Allen's information up on the screen, so I asked for his full name and date of birth just to make sure. "It's Gregory A. Allen, d.o.b.

151

01/17/54," Mark said. I compared it with middle initial and date of birth of the Gregory Allen named in the criminal complaint that I'd found in the Avery file – it was the same guy. And then a sinking, sickening feeling that would return with varying degrees of intensity over the next few weeks came over me.

After Sherry hung up, Mark and I delved further into Gregory Allen's past. CCAP revealed that by the time he assaulted Penny Beerntsen in 1985, Allen had already chalked up a considerable record. And worse, because he wasn't charged with assaulting Penny, Allen not only had a past – he had a future too. Sherry Culhane had alluded to it. On June 27, 1995, ten years after he avoided prosecution for assaulting Penny Beerntsen, Allen broke into a residence on the north side of Green Bay and raped the woman inside while the woman's daughter lay sleeping in a room near-by. He was convicted of kidnapping, burglary, and second degree sexual assault "while possessing a bulletproof garment," and the presiding judge sent him away for sixty years.

The records also revealed that while he was in custody awaiting trial for the Green Bay assault, authorities in South Carolina issued a Fugitive Complaint asking the State of Wisconsin to return him to South Carolina once the prosecution here was complete. He was wanted on "suspicion of murder" for a crime that occurred in the 1970s. That complaint was later dismissed, but regardless, Allen was one scary dude.

Mark and I gathered our thoughts and started, as the saying goes, "to think like lawyers." By nature, lawyers are creatures of caution. It's our job to look ahead and imagine every possible way something might go wrong, and then make sure it doesn't. We take nothing for granted, and knowing that if we miss anything, the consequences could be dire, we double-check everything.

If Avery was innocent, we'd have to get him released – that much was obvious. But before taking such a momentous step, we had to be certain that the Crime Lab's finding meant what it seemed to mean. The DNA results appeared to show that Gregory Allen was the assailant, not Steven Avery, but you never know. After all, a jury had found Avery guilty and the Court of Appeals had twice upheld his conviction. Before undoing all that on the strength of microscopic evidence on one pubic hair, we better be sure.

So we split the file in half. Mark would focus on the physical evidence by reviewing the police and crime lab reports, and I would read the trial transcript to see what other evidence the State had presented at trial. The idea was to see how the DNA results on the hair squared with the rest of the evidence, and who knows – maybe the reports would suggest some other physical evidence that could be tested for DNA.

Mark soon discovered that Denis Vogel had presented precious little physical evidence at trial, and what he did present was of questionable scientific validity and almost no probative value for the jury – in fact, it was junk. Vogel tried to link Avery to the crime, literally by a hair – though it might just as well have been a thread, when he employed the "science" of hair examination to suggest that a hair recovered from Avery's shirt was that of the victim. Even though she'd been called by the prosecution, Sherry Culhane took pains to spell out the limited usefulness of hair examination.

"Is it possible to prove identification by hair analysis?" Jim Bolgert had asked.

"No," Culhane candidly replied.

"Is the hair of many people consistent with each other?"

"Yes."

"Can you give an opinion as to the probability whether the two hairs are from the same source?"

"No."

"All you can say is that it's not impossible that they're from the same source, isn't that correct?"

"That's right."

It's not the job of the scientists at the Crime Lab to win convictions for the State, and when Sherry Culhane worked on the Avery case in 1985, she did just what she should have: she used the tools of science available at the time to objectively analyze the physical evidence, and then she testified truthfully about the results. When she told the jury that the hair found on Avery's shirt was consistent with the hair of the victim, "consistency" meant something less than ninety percent certain. So it isn't surprising that in the years following Avery's trial, hair examination lost whatever meager standing it previously held in the scientific community, and even before the advent of DNA, most courts throughout the nation ruled it inadmissible.

Eighteen years later, still working at the crime lab, Culhane remained the analyst assigned to this case, and it was she who isolated the DNA on the pubic hair that set Avery free. But this time the odds weren't one in ten – this time they were 1 in 251 billion.

Having satisfied himself that Vogel's hair evidence was bogus, Mark shifted gears. He kept his eyes open for any other physical evidence that the prosecution hadn't used at trial that might point to Avery's involvement despite the new DNA finding. There wasn't any. Then he meticulously reviewed the file to confirm that the pubic hair containing Allen's DNA was linked by an ironclad chain of custody all the way back to 1985. It was.

* * *

Meanwhile, I started reviewing the trial transcript, deciding late that afternoon to take it home. It was going to be a long night, and I knew I'd much rather spend it at home with Jody and the kids than in the modestly furnished gray surroundings of my government office.

I kicked one of the boys off my favorite living room chair and then I dove back into the Avery trial, plowing my way through the transcript and jotting down a few notes along the way.

I've prosecuted my fair share of sex assaults over the years, but I was struck by the brutality of this one – by the way the assailant shook the victim so violently that her head slammed into the ground, and by how she crawled toward the water for help after he left, sitting there naked on the beach, dazed, and staring at her blood-soaked hands. I was also impressed by the strength of her character, both in withstanding the assault and in recounting it to the jury six months later.

But I was surprised by how conspicuous the DA's appeal to emotion was. A trial is supposed to be about getting at the truth, at least for the prosecutor, and since it's through the mind and not the heart that the truth is generally found, prosecutors are supposed to use emotion sparingly. In fact, before deliberations, jurors are specifically instructed not to be swayed by sympathy or passion in reaching their verdict, but to be guided by reason and judgment instead.

Apparently, Denis Vogel didn't subscribe to that view of prosecution. Having the victim and her husband re-enact the assault in front of the jury wasn't just bad taste, it was disingenuous overkill. And the crime-scene re-enactment with the victim up to her knees in the water while a coast guard chopper snapped a few photographs from the sky was ridiculous. These dramatic courtroom stunts shed no light

155

whatsoever on the question at hand. The issue wasn't whether the assault occurred, or even how it was accomplished – it was whether Steven Avery was the assailant.

I became increasingly confident as I continued reading the transcript that the DNA results meant exactly what they appeared to mean, that Steven Avery was innocent. So my focus shifted to how the Sheriff and the DA could have been so certain that Avery was the assailant – and I didn't like what I found.

"What's with the greasy hands?" I almost said out loud. Avery's wife and his mother both testified that his hands were permanently greasy because he worked on cars every day, and it was impossible to get them clean. The clerk at the ShopKo in Green Bay even noticed how greasy his hands were when he and his wife went through the check-out line. Every cop in the county knew it. The Avery boys worked on cars all the time and their hands were perpetually greasy, and I'm sure Dvorak and Kocourek knew it too.

But when Deputy Dvorak and the Sheriff asked Penny Beerntsen at the hospital if the assailant's hands were greasy, she was adamant, "no, the man's hands weren't greasy, they were clean." Her answer was the same a few days later when Dvorak re-interviewed her at home. "The assailant's hands weren't greasy," she repeated, "as a matter of fact, the man smelled clean."

I looked up from the transcript. Whoever attacked Penny Beerntsen didn't have greasy hands and apparently Steven Avery always had greasy hands. *Shouldn't they have paused and considered that maybe it wasn't adding up before they went out and arrested him*, I thought. *And shouldn't the jury have paused before they found him guilty?*

I kept reading, and when I got to Gene Kusche's testimony, I was surprised with his meager qualifications as a police artist. He attended a course on "rapid visual perception" at the FBI Academy in Quantico, Virginia just six months before the trial. The course was designed to train cops to teach bank tellers and others in positions likely to witness crimes to better observe facial characteristics, so they could accurately describe offenders to the police. It included a two hour class described by Kusche as "an introduction" to drawing composite sketches. That introductory course was the only training Kusche ever received for the difficult art of drawing composite sketches, and as it turned out, the sketch in this case was the only one he ever completed that was introduced at trial.

Something else about the composite sketch didn't sound right. During cross-examination, Kusche conceded that it's not standard procedure to have a photo of a potential suspect before preparing a composite drawing. But Sheriff Kocourek had the jail bring Avery's mug shot up to the hospital more than an hour before Kusche started working on the sketch – the sketch that ended up looking exactly like Avery's mug shot. The reason they had one in this case, Kusche said, was because they already "had some idea who it might be." He also admitted that someone mentioned Avery's name before he started working on the sketch, but he claimed he didn't know who Avery was, even though he'd worked with his uncle for years. Also, several deputies were told more than two hours before Kusche finished the sketch to get ready to pick up Avery.

Gene Kusche is no longer with us, but when he was, he was a joy to be around. I remember how he'd greet me in Russian – "Mikhail!" he'd say in his booming Scottish voice, and then continue with some well-worn Russian phrase that he thought sounded impressive. But that night I wondered how he drew such a perfect likeness of Avery, one that looked exactly like Avery's mug shot, and as I kept plowing through the transcript, my suspicion only grew.

Penny Beerntsen initially told Deputy Dvorak that her assailant had brown eyes, but after she picked out the blue-eyed Steven Avery in the photo array and handed the photo to the Sheriff, she said, "I was mistaken, his eyes are blue."

And then there was the creepy telephone call that she received a few days after the assault. I've seen it before – fixated on the woman he assaulted, the assailant calls her a few days later to extend the nightmare and victimize her all over again. Or sometimes the call is to intimidate her so she won't cooperate with the police. It sounded to me like that kind of call, but it couldn't have been Avery – he was locked up in jail with strict orders from the Sheriff forbidding any calls.

My astonishment only grew when I got to Jim Bolgert's presentation of the defense. Not only was the State's evidence flimsy, but the defendant's alibi was incredibly strong. Even though Avery and his wife hadn't spoken, they gave the investigators the same detailed account of their day. So did his mom and dad. In fact, there were more than ten witnesses who testified that Avery couldn't have done it – he was with them at the Salvage Yard that day. Five of them claimed they saw him after *Divorce Court* ended at three-thirty, just twenty minutes before the assault began fifteen miles down the road and a half mile up the sand from the parking lot at Neshotah Park. The Defense also presented a receipt from ShopKo that established Avery was in Green Bay at 5:13 pm, which virtually proved he didn't commit the assault. *How the hell did this happen*, I thought to myself, *why did the prosecution go through with it, and how did the jury vote to convict?*

But at the same time, I couldn't help but be impressed with Denis Vogel's trial skills – how he used the brutality of the assault to engender sympathy for the victim and disgust for whoever assaulted her.

It was after midnight when I went to bed that night, but the thousand plus pages of trial testimony were swirling around in my head and I couldn't fall asleep. When you try a case, you live and breathe it, and after awhile you come to know the truth. I hadn't tried the case but I felt like I had, and I couldn't imagine how Denis Vogel could have thought Avery was guilty. Unless there was something Mark found out in his review of the physical evidence, there was no doubt that Avery had been wrongfully convicted, and tomorrow morning we'd have to begin the process of cutting him loose. I hoped that would be the end of it. But I knew it wouldn't be.

* * *

Mark and I compared notes first thing the following morning. We were both satisfied that Avery was innocent, at least of this particular crime, and we'd have to release him. But Mark suggested that we check a few other things first. He would call Sherry Culhane and ask her to run a second DNA test just to make sure, and I'd call Keith Findley at the Wisconsin Innocence Project to discuss a timeframe for Avery's release.

By the time I called him, Keith had already told Avery the good news. He was anxious for his client's release, but he also understood our need for caution. I think he also appreciated the non-adversarial way that Mark and I were handling the case. Of course his client was anxious to be released – he'd been in prison for eighteen years for a crime he didn't commit. But Keith said he would tell Avery they had to wait until the DNA results were confirmed – it shouldn't take more than a week.

Keith also agreed to put a muzzle on his client's family until the new DNA test confirmed his innocence. We all knew there'd be a media-frenzy as soon as word of the exoneration got out, and everyone wanted to have their ducks in a row before the madness began.

Mark wanted to check one other thing just to make sure. We needed to confirm that Gregory Allen wasn't in jail or prison somewhere on the day Penny Beerntsen was assaulted. So we called the Department of Corrections. Allen had served a stint in prison on a burglary conviction a few years earlier, but on the day Penny was attacked, he was roaming the streets. Or more accurately, he was prowling the sands.

* * *

Penny Beerntsen was about to learn that the man she believed assaulted her, the man who spent the last eighteen years in prison on the strength of her identification, was innocent. It wasn't going to be easy for her – in fact, it would be miserable.

I already knew Penny, so it made sense that I'd be the one to call her with the news. She told me that summer she repeatedly tried reaching Jim Fitzgerald and shared with me her frustration that he wasn't returning her calls. She knew the Court had ordered the hairs re-tested, but that was four months earlier, and since then, she'd been left in the dark. This was around the same time it was discovered that the stickers had apparently fallen off the exhibits.

Someone told me that Janine Geske had called our office several months earlier inquiring about the status of the Avery case. Geske had previously served as a Justice on the Wisconsin Supreme Court, but several years earlier she decided not to seek re-election and now she was teaching law at Marquette University in Milwaukee. Janine and Penny met through their work in the restorative justice program in the Wisconsin prison system, and during the last few years, she had been helping Penny navigate the legal and the emotional

160

ups and downs of the Avery case. Mostly, though, they were good friends, and I thought she'd have some ideas about how best to break the news.

So I called Janine and told her about the DNA test results. Like all of us, she was shocked by the news. She said Penny would be devastated, that she'd blame herself and would be sickened that an innocent man spent eighteen years in prison. She was especially concerned about Gregory Allen and the possibility that he was in attendance at one of the restorative justice classes that Penny helped facilitate in prison. So she asked if I could check which prisons Gregory Allen was incarcerated in during the preceding six years. If we could establish that he hadn't attended one of their presentations, she could at least put that fear out of Penny's mind. She also asked if I could get a hold of a mug shot of Gregory Allen, the closer to the date of the assault, the better. Penny would want to see what her real assailant looked like. She'd need to see his face.

At the end of our conversation, I asked Janine if it wouldn't be better if she told Penny about Avery's innocence rather than me. I knew she would eventually want to speak with someone in our office and I was more than happy to do so, but given their friendship, didn't it make more sense for her to break the news. I think Janine was thinking the same thing, and she promptly agreed. She told me she'd think about how best to tell Penny and she'd call me back to let me know how it went.

Janine called me back the next day. She tried calling Penny, but she and Tom were out of town for the weekend, so she left an innocuous message and asked Penny to call her when she returned. Her plan was to drive up to Manitowoc Sunday night to tell her in person instead. We couldn't keep the story under wraps much longer, so she'd have Penny get out of town before the media picked up the story. Janine would be her spokesperson.

Mark and I spent the next day hustling down the information that Janine Geske had requested. First on the agenda was finding out whether Allen could have been present during one of Penny and Janine's restorative justice classes. Tracing where Allen was housed wouldn't be easy. With the help of the Republican-dominated state legislature, Governor Tommy Thompson had spearheaded all sorts of tough-on-crime legislation during the 1990's, and with a steady stream of new offenders flowing into the system, business was booming for the prison industry. The State built new prisons as fast as it could, but the number of inmates grew so rapidly that they ran out of room and had to send some offenders as far away as Texas and Oklahoma. We knew that Allen would have been shuffled from one prison to the next – he could have been anywhere.

But we shouldn't have fretted. With the assistance of a committed records clerk at the Department of Corrections, we were able to track Allen's whereabouts from the day he was processed at Dodge Correctional in 1996 all the way to his current location. The news was good. After six months at Dodge, they shipped him from one prison to the next, but Allen was never housed at a prison on the same day Penny Beerntsen was there. It would be small comfort, but it was better than the alternative.

Next on the list was trying to find a mug shot of Allen from 1985. Mark and I went over to the Sheriff's Department – maybe they'd have one on file. Sure enough, Dispatch found one from a March 11, 1984 arrest. It was almost a year and a half before Penny's assault, but it was the best they could do. Allen was listed at 5'10" and 210 pounds. Notations indicated he had scars on his nose and his forehead. He listed his occupation as a sheet metal mechanic, and the "remarks" section noted, "Can be violent."

Janine called a few days later to tell me how it went with Penny. The news wasn't good. She said Penny was struggling with a swirl of emotions – guilt, sadness, anger, and fear. In a way, it was worse than the assault itself. At least she could kick and scratch to fight off the assailant, but there wasn't a thing she could do about Steven Avery's wrongful conviction.

Penny and Tom flew out to Colorado where their son lived in order to avoid the coming media storm and just to be alone for awhile, but Janine gave me their telephone number and suggested I give Penny a call. She needed confidence that the current DA's Office was on top of the situation and was interested in doing the right thing.

So I called the resort where the Beerntsens were staying, and we had a long conversation. Janine was right – Penny was devastated. I apologized on behalf of the office and told her this never should have happened. I must have told her ten times that it wasn't her fault.

She confided that after the trial she occasionally had doubts about Avery's guilt, especially during the appeals process when his attorneys kept relentlessly attacking his conviction. She mentioned that a week after the assault she received a telephone call from a detective at the Manitowoc Police Department. The detective told her that the city police department had a suspect in mind that matched the description of the assailant, and it wasn't Steven Avery. So she called the Sheriff's Department – she thought she spoke directly with Sheriff Kocourek – and told him about her conversation with the detective and asked him if there was another suspect. She was told not to concern herself with what the detective had told her – the Sheriff's Department had jurisdiction over the case, not the city PD.

* * *

Sherry Culhane had the results of the second DNA test in less than a week, just like she said she would. The test confirmed it – the pubic hair was Gregory Allen's, or at least there was only a 1 in 251 billion chance that it wasn't. Keith Findley drafted a Stipulation and Order vacating the conviction and dismissing the charges. Its concluding sentence was music to Avery's ears: "It is further ordered that Steven A. Avery shall be released from custody of the Wisconsin Department of Corrections forthwith." Mark and I signed the stipulation and walked it down to Branch 3 for Judge Hazlewood's signature.

News travels fast in courthouses – it always has and always will. So it wasn't a surprise that word about Steven Avery's exoneration was soon on the lips of every other person in the Courthouse. And the news was naturally the chief topic of discussion in the DA's office. A few members of our staff were already working here when Penny Beerntsen was assaulted in 1985, and the Victim-Witness Coordinator had gotten to know her during the course of the trial. We all talked about how horrible it would be for Penny. It would be all over the media and she'd have to re-live the whole ordeal nearly two decades after it happened. The degree of sympathy for Avery, on the other hand, varied from one person to the next. But about one matter we were unanimous – Steven Avery would be even more messed up now than he was when he went in.

Another thing about courthouses is that the people who work in them aren't afraid to speak their minds. As I said, two of the women in our office were already working in the DA's office when Denis Vogel prosecuted Avery back in 1985, and a

164

third still worked for the County but in a different capacity. None of them thought Avery was the assailant. In fact, each of them thought Gregory Allen was. Allen had been in and out of Court during the preceding six months for stalking, window peeping, and stealing women's underwear – not the types of offenses that go unnoticed by women who work in prosecutor's offices.

As the Victim-Witness Coordinator, Brenda Petersen frequently worked with detectives from the various police agencies within the County. Brenda recalled that during the summer Penny Beerntsen was assaulted, the Manitowoc Police Department was keeping a close eye on Gregory Allen, and while the Avery case was pending, some of the detectives were convinced that it was Allen, not Avery, who assaulted Penny Beerntsen. Brenda also said she watched the entire trial, and she never believed Avery was the assailant.

In fact, Brenda and two other staff members were so concerned that Allen was the assailant that they went into Denis Vogel's office and told him so. But Vogel said it was impossible. He said that Allen was on probation in Door County, and his agent said he was in Sturgeon Bay at the time of the assault. Nope, Vogel said, it couldn't have been Allen. He had an alibi.

Later, a Department of Justice independent investigation would find out otherwise. Gregory Allen wasn't on probation on the day Penny Beerntsen was assaulted, like Denis Vogel said he was. The "sand-man," as some of the officers had taken to calling Allen, was free to roam the beach and terrorize his next victim. Incidentally, Vogel told the Department of Justice investigators that he didn't "specifically recall" anyone from his office commenting about the Avery case, though he admitted his staff frequently discussed cases.

* * *

It was impossible to keep the story under wraps any longer. The news outlets would soon catch wind of Avery's pending release from prison and the "you-know-what" would hit the fan. So with the help of a more erudite courthouse lawyer, Mark and I whipped up a press release and faxed it to the local newspaper and TV stations in Milwaukee and Green Bay. After covering the essentials, we tried to put the best spin on Avery's exoneration:

> Upon receipt of the new DNA evidence, this office conducted an exhaustive review of the original investigation, earlier crime lab reports, and the complete court record. Based upon this review, it is clear that Steven Avery did not commit this crime. It is tragic that Mr. Avery spent eighteen years in prison for a crime he did not commit, but the DNA identification technology that has exonerated Mr. Avery was not available when this case was investigated and prosecuted in 1985. Now that technological advances have established that Mr. Avery did not commit this crime, justice requires the dismissal of the charges, and it is my duty to see that Mr. Avery is immediately released from prison.

Clear blue autumn skies and comfortably mild temperatures greeted Steven Avery on the morning he was released. Television and print reporters flocked to Stanley Correctional Institute in northwestern Wisconsin at the appointed time and mobbed the protagonist as he walked out a free man.

Here's how reporter Tom Kertscher of the *Milwaukee Journal Sentinel* covered the story:

Under a bright sun just before 9 a.m. Thursday morning, Steven Avery took his final steps toward freedom with his sister on one arm and his daughter on the other, his parents and his history-making legal team trailing behind.

There was a pause as the group approached the final set of locked doors at the prison. More than 17 years behind bars for a wrongly convicted man were about to end.

"I'm out!" the soft-spoken Avery cried. "Feels wonderful."

Moments later, the 41-year-old former auto salvage worker became the first Wisconsin inmate to get his conviction overturned by the Wisconsin Innocence Project and only the third state inmate to be freed from prison through DNA testing.

A day after the testing proved that another man had beaten and sexually assaulted a Manitowoc woman in 1985 Avery expressed no anger toward the victim, who had repeatedly identified him as her attacker.

"It ain't her fault," he stated simply, directing blame instead at the Manitowoc County Sheriff's Department for making him a suspect. "They put it mostly in her head."

The Sheriff's Department, in Avery's estimation, didn't want to pursue other leads once it had helped steer the victim toward identifying him. He claimed that after his arrest the sheriff told him he would never get bail and never get out of jail.

"They wanted somebody real bad," he said. "And I was the one."

But while expressing sympathy for Avery, Tom Kocourek, who was sheriff in Manitowoc County when Avery was arrested, defended his department's investigation of the case and called his conviction "unfortunate".

"I don't know what else we could have done at the time," he said.

Trying not to dwell on the case, Avery was cheered Thursday by the presence of one of his five children, 19-year-old Jennifer. But he shed tears over how his conviction led quickly to the end of his marriage and the estrangement of his twin sons, now 18, who were born six days before his arrest.

"There ain't no way I can make it up," Avery said of the time he lost with his family.

But after spending some time with his parents, Avery said he plans to settle in Crivitz, near where most of his children live. He urged other wrongly convicted prisoners to remain faithful.

"There's always miracles going around," he said. "Hopefully they can get out just like me and get the guilty one in."

* * *

Over the next few weeks the airwaves remained filled with news of Avery's exoneration, and time and again it was reported that he spent eighteen years in prison for a crime he didn't commit. But it wasn't eighteen years – it was only twelve; Avery had cut a deal on the other charges that were pending against him, the charges associated with his forcing the deputy's wife off the road. He was sentenced to six years for those charges, and even though the lesser sentence ran concurrent with the thirty-two years on the attempted murder and sexual assault charges, he still would have spent those six years in prison even if he wasn't wrongfully convicted of the other charges.

Still, whether he'd been locked up for eighteen years or twelve, it didn't matter – Steven Avery was a celebrity now. With his shaved head, twinkling blue eyes, and foot-long beard, the media loved him. And given all the attention they lavished upon him, and with a special affinity to attractive young female reporters, Avery loved them too.

Before long, everyone in Wisconsin knew his name, and given the number of television interviews he granted, most people recognized his face too. But what they didn't know, and what Avery himself didn't know, was that two years later he'd be at the center of a far greater media storm.

Steven Avery, with family, on his release from prison

EIGHTEEN

THE NEXT DAY WAS Friday, and it was a relief the work week would soon be over. I went for a run and then relaxed with a bottle of Miller that wasn't Lite.

I called it a night and went up to bed, but the beer didn't have the effect I'd hoped for. The discomfort I felt when I saw the Allen complaint in Vogel's file had returned over the past few days with varying degrees of intensity, and now the question was staring me straight in the eyes. Did they know? Did Vogel and Kocourek know that Gregory Allen was Penny's assailant?

I couldn't shake the feeling that something went horribly wrong back in 1985. Two summers before he assaulted Penny Beerntsen, Allen had lunged at another woman on the same beach who was walking her dog, and the criminal complaint charging him was in Vogel's file. Why was it there? Did it mean Vogel knew it was Allen and that Avery was innocent?

To answer the questions, I needed to find out more. So the next day at work I retrieved the police reports concerning Allen's earlier crime. Mark and I instinctively knew to leave them where I found them in the file in case somebody outside the office would later have to investigate, so we made copies and returned the originals to the file.

Reviewing the reports didn't make me feel any better – in fact, it only made it worse. The victim was walking her dog on the beach when a man wearing blue shorts and a tank top, who we now knew was Allen, suddenly ran over the sand dunes. He began walking behind her, and when he got close enough, he pulled his shorts half way down and began masturbating. Then he lunged for her, just like he lunged at Penny Beerntsen two summers later, but in this case, the victim was able to escape his grasp and run away.

The victim told police she recognized the man – he used to come into the convenience store where she worked, and a co-worker even knew his name. It was Gregory Allen. The woman called the police again a few days later. She was scared. Allen had called her twice. She'd moved to Green Bay, but Allen had her telephone number somehow, which meant he also knew where she lived.

I couldn't believe it. Allen used the exact same M.O. two years later when he assaulted Penny Beerntsen – right down to calling her after the crime. How could Vogel not make the connection? And if he didn't, why were the Allen reports in his file!

Then I looked at the criminal complaint. I was hoping Vogel just signed off on the complaint and someone else actually handled the prosecution, as frequently happens in DA offices. But that's not what I found. Vogel had personally prosecuted the file – from beginning to end. He appeared for the State at the bail hearing after Allen was arrested and successfully argued for $500 cash bail. He was the prosecutor at the pretrial conference, when he ironically noted in the file that "the defendant may have alibi." He subpoenaed the State's witnesses for trial, and he cut a plea agreement with the defense attorney a few days before the trial. And on February 28, 1984, with Gregory Allen in Court to enter his plea, Vogel amended the charge to disorderly conduct. The Judge adopted the plea agreement and ordered a fine of one hundred dollars plus costs – not a bad deal for dropping his drawers and accosting a woman on the beach.

* * *

Mark and I devoted much of our time to the Avery case in the first week after the Crime Lab called, but our regular caseload didn't disappear. The other attorneys in the office were swamped too, but they pitched in and somehow we muddled through. But bombshells were exploding every other day, and now it was time for another. Mark asked me to join him in his office, and by the look of his face I knew it was serious. One of the other prosecutors in the office had called Gene Kusche. Gene was retired by this time, but for some reason, our colleague called him about the Avery case. Mark caught wind of it and asked him what they discussed.

He said he called Kusche to see if he knew about Avery's exoneration and that he would soon be released from prison. Apparently, he thought Kusche should know about it before he found out through the media. Nobody's ever accused the two of them of being men of few words, so the conversation covered other ground too.

Kusche told the ADA about an incident that occurred ten years after Avery was convicted. A detective from Green Bay had called our jail to report that an inmate in their jail was claiming that he had raped a woman jogging on a beach in Manitowoc County ten years earlier. The inmate claimed that someone else had been convicted of the assault and was presently serving time in prison for a crime he didn't commit. Kusche told the ADA that Andy Colborn was the corrections officer who spoke with the Green Bay detective and that Colborn got word of it to Sheriff Kocourek. But according to Kusche, the Sheriff told Colborn and a detective to stay out of it – they already had the right guy. Andy Colborn doesn't recall if the Green Bay detective mentioned the confessing inmate's name, but Gregory Allen was in the Brown County jail at the time awaiting trial for raping the woman in Green Bay ten years after he had attacked Penny Beerntsen on the beach.

Kusche told the assistant DA something else that was even more disturbing. He said he withdrew the composite drawing from the court file several years earlier. It was at his home, and he was planning to keep it there.

It went right over my head then, but Penny Beerntsen said something similar during our phone conversation a few days earlier. She told me she ran into Kusche a few years back at the grocery store, and he said something odd, something that really disturbed her at the time. He said he had the composite drawing from the Avery trial hanging on his living room wall, and asked her if she wanted to come over to see it. Naturally, Penny was creeped out by his offer and she politely declined. And now, Kusche just told one of my colleagues that he still has the composite drawing and he plans to hold onto it. What the hell was going on?

Nobody removes evidence from a court file without permission of the Judge, not even cops, so I assumed Judge Hazlewood must have released the drawing to Kusche. Later that day I checked, and sure enough, on October 14, 1998, thirteen years after Steven Avery's trial, the Judge signed an order releasing the composite drawing to Inspector Kusche. The order also released the original of Avery's mug shot that was moved into evidence at trial, the one that Penny picked out from the photo array that night in the hospital.

I suppose Kusche looked at the composite drawing as a trophy – his masterpiece that helped send a dangerous pervert to prison. But it still struck me as odd. Trophies are for sports competitions, not for attempted murder trials.

* * *

Another bombshell exploded a few days later. In the summer of 1989, a professional snitch by the name of Ray Crivitz was serving time at the state prison in Green Bay when he struck up a conversation with an inmate in the adjoining cell. The inmate went by the name of "Stivers," but his real name was Steven Avery. Crivitz memorialized their dreary conversation in the following sworn affidavit, dated June 14, 2000, eleven years after the conversation supposedly occurred:

AFFIDAVIT OF RAYMOND E. CRIVITZ:

I, Raymond E. Crivitz, do hereby swear and attest to the following:

1.   My name is Raymond E. Crivitz.
2.   As of the date of the signing of this affidavit, I am an inmate at Green Bay Correctional Institution in Green Bay, Wisconsin.
3.   During a previous period of my incarceration I lived here from fall of 1988 to the summer of 1989.
4.   During this period of incarceration I was housed in the North Cell Hall, C Tier, in cell C-73.

5.   While I was living in C-73, I came to know another inmate who was housed in C-72 right next to my cell.

6.   This inmate was Steve Avery (approximately 5'5" tall with sandy/dirty blond hair and ice blue eyes), who also went by the nickname "Stivers."

7.   During one of several conversations I had with Steve Avery (while each of us were sitting in our cells), in the spring/summer of 1989, I asked him what he was in for.

8.   Steve Avery told me that he was arrested and convicted for raping a woman on a beach near Manitowoc, WI.

9.   I responded that I was also in for assault (even though I wasn't) just to get his trust and so he would talk to me.

10.   Steve Avery told me that he was "set up by this bitch," that he was on the beach and saw a woman jogging. He said he "wanted some." I asked him if he got some.

11.   Steve Avery then told me that "yes he got some," that he "fucked the bitch" and that "she loved it."

12.   I asked him if that was a small town and if he thought he would see her again. He said it was and that if he did see her again that he "would finish what he started" because he felt he had been "set up by the bitch" and that he thought she was working with the police or was some kind of policewoman.

13.   About three weeks later I was transferred out of Green Bay Correctional Institution.

Here's the strange part: Sheriff Kocourek kept a safe in his office, and Crivitz's affidavit was the only thing left in it when the new Sheriff, Ken Petersen, took over from Kocourek in 2001. Petersen sent Mark a copy of Crivitz's affidavit that morning.

To me, it sounded like Avery was engaging in typical inmate bravado to an equally typical jailhouse snitch. Crivitz even wrote in paragraph nine that he told Avery he was in for assault even though he wasn't, "just to get his trust," and Avery was very likely doing the same thing. That's *if* the conversation even occurred.

But why was the affidavit the only thing left in the Sheriff's safe? Did he really believe Avery was guilty and held onto the affidavit in case he had to prove it? But why hide it? Why not add it to a follow-up police report and send a copy to the DA – that would be standard procedure, and Tom Kocourek is certainly a standard procedure kind of guy. Or was it his trump card? If the truth ever came out, he could hold up the affidavit and say, "Look, I thought he did it."

Who knows? But what we do know is that the affidavit was prepared eleven years after the conversation supposedly occurred, and Sheriff Kocourek kept it securely hidden in a safe. It was just one more odd fact in a series of increasingly odd facts in a case that was becoming more disturbing by the day.

* * *

As Mark and I learned more about the circumstances surrounding Avery's wrongful conviction, it felt like we were in the middle of a storm. Events were beginning to spin out of control. Each revelation was more disturbing than the previous one, and taken together, they suggested that Kocourek and Vogel might have knowingly sent an innocent man to prison while letting a guilty one go free. We knew we had to get a handle on it. Someone would eventually have to investigate this mess, and it sure as hell wasn't going to be us – there was an obvious conflict of interest. So the following day Mark put out what he referred to as a "gag order":

Date: September 11, 2003

To: The Entire Office
From: District Attorney Mark Rohrer

Re: Steven Avery Case

Effective immediately, I am issuing the following directive: No one is to discuss this case with anyone outside this office. Any inquiries about this case should be directed to me. The basis of this directive is due to the sensitive nature of this case. Thank you for your cooperation on this directive.

We called the Attorney General's office in Madison late that afternoon to see if they would conduct an independent review. We didn't know it at the time, but Keith Findley of the Innocence Project had made the same request. But citing what she perceived to be an absence of legal authority to conduct such an investigation, Attorney General Peg Lautenschlager declined. Then, less than a week later, she changed her mind. She had recently rolled out the brand new "Public Integrity Unit," and she belatedly decided that Avery's wrongful conviction was just the sort of case the initiative was designed for.

When Mark and I drove to Madison that morning, the Avery case was already on its way to becoming the most notorious wrongful conviction in Wisconsin's history. The state's major newspapers ran several front page stories about the exoneration, and the electronic media continued to saturate

177

the airwaves with coverage of every new development. It was also the subject of an AM radio talk show out of Milwaukee. We couldn't escape it.

Actually, the coverage was quite good. "Quick Action in Avery Case May Have Left Man Free to Continue Crimes," read the headline in the *Milwaukee Journal Sentinel* the day before. Reporter Tom Kertscher informed his readers that even though Gregory Allen was convicted of lunging at a woman along the same beach two summers earlier, the police apparently never considered him a suspect in the second assault. Kertscher also noted that because Allen wasn't arrested for assaulting Penny Beerntsen, he was free ten years later to break into a Green Bay woman's home and brutally rape her.

One of the Green Bay TV stations ran a segment about the Avery case the night before, complete with a live interview of the protagonist himself, on location at the Avery Salvage Yard. With his long hair and scraggly beard hanging half way down to his belly button, Avery affected a Mansonesque appearance during his years in prison. But now he was all cleaned up. He kept the mangy beard, but his hair was buzzed and his icy blue eyes twinkled like Santa Claus.

Steve told the reporter he wasn't angry at anybody for his plight. He just hoped an investigation would be conducted so nobody else would have to go through what he did. For the time being he planned to live with his parents, and, oh yeah, he was keeping his options open about filing a lawsuit.

I picked up the latest edition of the *Journal Sentinel* when Mark stopped to gas up half way to Madison, and the Avery case made the front page again. "Manitowoc County DA Requests Avery Case Review – Wants the Attorney General to Look for Safeguards," read the headline of that day's installment.

Kertscher had contacted some of the players involved. Mark's pretty tight-lipped with the press, so after noting his request for an independent review, he told the reporter he couldn't comment further on the case because he wanted "to ensure the integrity of any independent review." Denis Vogel was identified as the former District Attorney who prosecuted the case, but Vogel couldn't be reached for comment.

Avery, on the other hand, was more than willing to talk to the reporter. He thought the police suspected him because he had a few run-ins with the law, he explained, and the Sheriff's Department didn't like him. Also, his uncle Arland was a deputy at the Sheriff's Department, and so was one of his neighbors. He claimed the Sheriff told him after he was arrested that he wouldn't be admitted to bail and that he'd never get out of jail.

Surprisingly, Sheriff Kocourek also agreed to be interviewed. Here's that part of the story:

> Sheriff Tom Kocourek, who retired in 2001, called Avery's conviction 'unfortunate'. But he expressed confidence that his department had aggressively pursued all leads and that the 'vast majority' of evidence had pointed to Avery. 'I don't know what else we could have done at the time,' he said. 'We didn't leave any stones unturned.'

The article concluded by noting that according to the New York-based national Innocence Project Steven Avery was the 137th wrongfully convicted person in the United States to be freed from prison through DNA testing.

* * *

The city of Madison lies on an isthmus between Lake Monona and Lake Mendota. But while Madison isn't quite an island geographically, it may as well be, given its politics and cultural identity. As the State's Capitol and home to its largest university, the city is filled with lawyers and university professors who can seem foreign to the rest of the state which, with the exception of Milwaukee and a few other hold-outs from the days of "Fighting Bob" La Follette, tends to vote red.

Mark and I arrived in Madison three hours after leaving Manitowoc, just in time for our 10 a.m. appointment with the Attorney General. I'd met Peg Lautenschlager before and she warmly greeted us before we got down to business. She introduced us to Deb Straus and Amy Blackwood-Lehman, the two special agents she'd assigned to handle the investigation.

We walked into a conference room where ten to fifteen agents and attorneys were waiting to grill us about why we were there. But it didn't take long to see that they were interested in the case, and they asked intelligent and insightful questions that showed they cared. We walked out two hours later, confident that the Attorney General's Office would conduct a fair and thorough investigation, which is all anybody could ask for.

After leaving the AG's Office we walked up State Street, which runs between the Capitol building and the University. We had lunch at an Afghan restaurant, then walked back to the Capitol building and wandered through its maze of hallways in search of Representative Mark Gundrum's office. A Republican legislator from suburban Milwaukee and the chairman of the State Assembly's Committee on Courts and Corrections, Gundrum had called for hearings two days earlier to explore what led to Avery's wrongful conviction. He must have caught wind that Mark had requested an independent investigation because he called the previous day to see if we'd stop by after our meeting with the Attorney General.

We weren't sure how much to share with Representative Gundrum. For one thing, we didn't want to say anything that would compromise the Attorney General's investigation. But also, the Democrat Peg Lautenschlager and the Republican Mark Gundrum were both ambitious politicians, and we weren't interested in becoming pawns in a political chess match between the two of them.

So when we arrived at Gundrum's office, we expected to be met by a self-serving politician who was hoping to make some political hay out of Avery's wrongful conviction. But instead, we were pleasantly surprised. It was clear from the start that Gundrum actually cared. He was knowledgeable about the criminal justice system in general and sincerely concerned about how in this case it had so miserably failed. The State Assembly eventually heeded his call for hearings, and Gundrum was appointed the chairperson of what would later, if temporarily, come to be known as the Avery Task Force. By all accounts, he did an excellent job.

* * *

Mark and I had beaten a few more dead horses discussing the Avery case on our way home from Madison when I began nodding off. I just finished reading the latest article about the case in the Manitowoc *Herald Times Reporter* when, despite having consumed the 24 oz. cup of coffee that I picked up on our way out of town, I fell into a deep sleep. The reporter had covered the same ground as the *Journal Sentinel* piece did. Mark's request for an independent review was there, along with a few interviews of some of the main players. But it was a quote from Steven Avery himself that, had I not been half asleep when I read it, would have jolted me from my seat.

Avery claimed in the article that Gene Kusche drew the composite sketch off his mug shot, the one the Sheriff's Department had on file from his arrest six months before Penny Beerntsen's assault. He told the reporter that one of his relatives told him so, which I assumed at the time and later confirmed, was his uncle Arland.

I'd heard from several people by then that the composite drawing looked suspiciously like Avery's mug shot. In fact, I'd been told, they were nearly identical. But seeing it in print gave the claim an authenticity that it had previously lacked – even though it was Avery who was making the claim. Now it was a public accusation, an allegation the newspaper gave enough credence to that they felt comfortable putting it in print. It was no longer just a few insiders who wondered about the composite drawing, it was front page news and soon it would be all over town. Did Gene Kusche really forge the composite drawing? I was staggered by the possibility and desperately worried that it was true.

* * *

It was one of the strangest telephone conversations I've ever had. Judge Hazlewood had suggested several days earlier that I call Denis Vogel to tell him about the DNA results so he'd have time to digest the news before the media started hounding him. That seemed reasonable, so I called him and told him about Avery's exoneration. Although we'd met on a few occasions, we didn't really know each other, so our conversation was short. Vogel wasn't surprised – and he didn't even try to fake it. He sent an innocent man to prison, but he wasn't a bit bothered by that fact, or if he was, he sure didn't show it.

Now it was the following Monday, and Vogel had left a message on my voice mail asking me to give him a call. I was in Court all morning, and he must have wanted something pretty bad because he called again that afternoon before I had a chance to return his call. Again, he was all business. He said an analyst from the Crime Lab had testified at the trial, and his recollection was that her examination of some hairs had tied Avery to the crime. *Yeah, right, Denis*, I thought, *you're still relying on the "science" of hair examination.* Then, almost nonchalantly, Vogel asked me a question I'll never forget: "Is there anything on Allen in the file?"

I feigned ignorance, and mumbled something inconsequential about the case instead. I told him Mark and I turned the file over to the Attorney General the previous Friday, which I'm sure wasn't news to him since the media had already extensively covered Mark's request for an independent review.

I hung up the phone and just sat there in my office for a minute or two, reflecting upon the conversation. Vogel's question about whether there was anything about Allen left in his file implied he knew that Allen, not Avery, was the assailant, didn't it? He was covering his behind, and he must have thought I'd go along. How else could I take it? Despite their reputation, most attorneys possess as much integrity as the next person, maybe even more, but Denis Vogel seemed to be one of the exceptions. How could he prosecute someone he knew was innocent? And how could he let somebody as dangerous as Allen go free?

But being sanctimonious is an occupational hazard for prosecutors, one I'm not immune from. So I tried to temper my judgment about what Vogel had done with an understanding of why he did it. *None of us is perfect*, I thought, *far from it.*

Part of the problem, I thought, was that by rushing the decision to arrest Avery without consulting Vogel, the Sheriff started a course of action that would be difficult to stop. I suppose Vogel could have cut him loose at the bail hearing and summoned him in later if he thought the case was strong enough to charge. But with such a prominent victim and with the media paying such close attention, letting Avery go free would have been politically difficult – after all, he had to run for re-election every two years. *Besides,* I thought for a moment, *it's possible he didn't know.*

But the more I tried to convince myself that Vogel didn't know, the more convinced I became he did. And the more I thought about why he did it, the more I realized there was nothing that could possibly justify it. Sure, he had to run for re-election, but you can't play politics with crime. And then I recalled what some of the staff in our office told me a few days earlier. From the very beginning they thought Allen, not Avery, was the assailant, but Vogel told them Allen had an alibi – which, like so much else in this case, turned out to be a lie.

NINETEEN

FORMER MANITOWOC POLICE Department Detective Tom Bergner was one of the good guys. He called me ADA, pronounced as one word beginning with a long 'a', because of the way I signed off on memos – ADA Griesbach. And since he was the deputy chief, I called him DC. Tom's retired now, but for years he was a great detective and then a great DC.

I called him the day after my strange telephone conversation with Denis Vogel to ask if he could do me a favor. I wanted to find out why Vogel's staff was so convinced that Gregory Allen was the assailant, and why he was so worried that something on Allen remained in his file. I didn't know how far back the department's records went, I said, but could he send me whatever he had from the last twenty five years that listed Allen as the suspect. Bergner uttered one of his more imaginative obscenity-laden insults and then replied, of course he could – he'd have the files on my desk later that day.

The records on Allen went back the full twenty-five years, and when I started reading them I couldn't believe my eyes. Steven Avery wasn't the only bad guy the cops were keeping their eyes on in the summer of 1985. In fact, he was a model citizen compared to what Allen was up to. It started in January of that year, and the police were just waiting for a strong enough case to bring him in.

At six-thirty in the morning on January 26, 1985, a woman on the south side of Manitowoc reported a suspicious man in her neighbor's back yard. The man had a ski mask on and it was still dark out, but she was able to see his outline as he moved a cement block brick underneath the neighbor's bathroom window, stood on the brick, and peered inside. Police later found out that the neighbor's teenage daughter was in the bathroom getting ready for school. She'd just gotten out of the shower when she looked outside and let out a scream.

The girl had told her parents a few weeks earlier that she had a strange feeling that someone was outside watching her when she was in the bathroom, but they didn't make much of it at the time – maybe it was just her imagination. But the man's face was right up to the window this time, and he was looking straight at her from out of the darkness. The girl managed to keep her wits about her long enough to remember what the man looked like, so she was able to give the police a good description. She picked out Gregory Allen from the photo array, and the police referred the case to the DA's office for prosecution. But an assistant DA sent it back a month later. He wouldn't be filing charges against Allen, he explained, because it was just a prowling incident, and in his opinion Allen's behavior didn't constitute a crime – though I'm not sure why at least disorderly conduct didn't come to mind. The city of Manitowoc had an ordinance that covered prowling, so the officer issued Allen a municipal court citation instead, although two months later the city attorney even dismissed that charge.

Untouched by the authorities, Gregory Allen remained on the prowl, striking usually just before sunrise. He was especially active in the months of June and July, when he engaged in increasingly violent and deranged behavior that culminated in his brutal assault of Penny Beerntsen on July 29.

His first victim that summer was 24-year-old Tina Hansen, who also lived on Manitowoc's south side. Tina kept late hours. As a bartender at the "Main Event," she didn't have a choice – in Wisconsin, closing time for taverns is at 2 a.m. At four-thirty in the morning on June 23, she was in her kitchen making posters for her parents' upcoming anniversary party. Nearly the longest day of the year, a faint morning light had already appeared when Tina heard tapping on her window. When she turned her head to look outside, she saw a man with a red tee-shirt wrapped around his head. His erect penis was exposed, and he was masturbating. It seemed like he was staring straight through her.

Her heart jumped – she'd left the front door open. She ran to lock it, but the man saw her and he ran too. She beat him there by seconds and quickly locked the screen door, but the man continued exposing himself and masturbating in front of her. He asked her to lift up her shirt to expose her breasts, a request she obviously denied.

"What difference would it make, you'll never see me again," the man pleaded.

"Get out of here, I'm calling the police," Tina yelled, hoping he'd leave. Then the man said he'd be back for more tomorrow, and then he scampered away.

Frightened, but not sure what to do, Tina waited ten minutes and then called the police. The responding officer advised her to call 911 immediately if the man returned.

A few days later than promised, but true to his word, the man struck again on June 26 at 2:31 am. Tina was sleeping

187

on a sofa this time when she heard knocking at the front door. The man with the red tee-shirt wrapped around his head had returned, and just like the first time, he exposed himself again. He had opened up the outside screen door to try to get in, but Tina screamed, and with his efforts frustrated for the second time in three days, the man fled.

Less than ten minutes after Tina's call into dispatch, an officer stopped Gregory Allen driving his motorcycle at 14th and Hamilton just four blocks from Tina's home. Allen was wearing a red tee-shirt, and other than having a mustache while Tina thought he was clean shaven, he matched her description. Tina discovered later that twelve Phillips screws had been removed from her bedroom window. Not coincidentally, Allen had two Phillips screw drivers in his possession when the officer stopped him earlier that morning.

The detective assembled a photo array that included a picture of Allen, and asked Tina if she recognized the man who twice appeared outside her home. Although she got a good look at Allen's eyes and his nose this time, the rest of his face was concealed by his tee-shirt so she wasn't able to identify him. But the detective was sure it was Allen, and alarmed at how reckless he'd become, he noted the following at the end of his report: "It would appear that this is getting very serious in regard to the suspect, Gregory A. Allen. He is in all probability the suspect involved, however, at this point the victim could not make a positive identification. Allen will have to be caught in the act as he is starting to become very bold."

It was getting serious alright. Just three weeks later, on July 14, 1985, Allen was the prime suspect in an even bolder crime.

Asleep, and alone in her south side residence, Megan Riley was only seventeen years old. Her parents were up north with her younger sister – they thought she'd be fine. But just after 3 a.m., she woke up to find a man holding a knife to her throat. It was impossible to identify him. With the exception of her one-piece bathing suit that had been hanging on the clothesline, but was now wrapped around his head, the intruder was nude.

"Say anything and I'll kill you," said the man, sitting on top of her now with one hand on her breast and the other over her mouth.

"Take off your clothes," he demanded, "Take off your clothes, or I'll kill you."

Megan pointed to the heating pad underneath her mid-section and managed to tearfully tell him she was having her period.

"Where's your younger sister," the man grunted, still sitting on top of her.

"Up north with my parents," she unwisely replied.

Then he put her hand on his penis and forced her to rub him until he ejaculated. After that, he took her by the arm, and with the knife to her throat again, he pushed her to the back door. "If you call the police I'll come back and kill you," the man said as he ran into the darkness, leaving as he entered – nude.

Megan hadn't noticed earlier, but when she looked down she noticed a stain on her nightgown where the man had ejaculated. Sick to her stomach, she threw up in the bathroom and then walked into the kitchen to settle herself down. She knew she had to move fast – what if he came back for some reason. She checked the phone, but it was dead. He must have cut the line. But she couldn't wait any longer, and after looking out every window to make sure he was gone, she made a dash to her car, locked the doors, and sped off to the police station.

Still shaking when the detective interviewed her thirty minutes later, she wasn't able to give a very good description. The man was about 5'8" with a solid build, she said, but that's all she knew. She thought he had a beard, but she wasn't even sure about that since he had her bathing suit wrapped around his head.

Determining the point of entry proved easy. The intruder had dragged a picnic table underneath the kitchen window, popped open the flimsy screen, and let himself in. A neighbor told the investigating officer that she saw a man park his motorcycle nearby at about two-thirty that morning and then walk toward Megan's house. She watched as the man carried a picnic bench between her house and Megan's. Another neighbor said he saw a man duck into the bushes in Megan's yard about a month earlier just before dark. He also noticed a motorcycle parked in front of a house nearby.

The police immediately suspected Gregory Allen. He had a motorcycle and the crime matched his MO, but without a better description, the investigation led nowhere, and a detective made the following entry at the end of the report: "This department has compiled several complaints recently concerning prowling, window peeping, indecent exposure, and sexual assault, ranging from January, 1985 through July 14, 1985. In each case, Gregory A. Allen has been listed as a suspect. Past record and intelligence concerning Gregory Allen reveals he is a dangerous individual with a potential for violence."

That note was entered on July 17, just twelve days before Penny Beerntsen was attacked and nearly murdered.

The Manitowoc PD began monitoring Allen's whereabouts, logging his location in an ongoing report. With each incident getting more serious than the last one, they knew he'd strike again – the only question was when. The log was included in the stack of reports that Tom Bergner had delivered to me, and as I examined them closely, I noted two entries for the day Allen attacked Penny Beerntsen. The first one indicated that Allen's motorcycle was at an address on the south side of town, and tragically, the second one merely stated: "Unable to check due to other calls."

And having escaped prosecution for attacking Penny Beerntsen, Allen was still up to no good three months later, a fact that should have given Vogel and Kocourek further pause, especially because his next crime was so similar to some of his prior shenanigans.

On October 17, with Steven Avery securely locked up in the county jail, police received a call from the concerned parents of two teenage girls. The girls, ages thirteen and fifteen, told them several times now that they saw "eyes looking at them" through the bathroom window in the early morning hours before it got light outside. The parents didn't know what to make of it – maybe the girls were just making up stories. But that morning the dad noticed a large block of wood underneath the bathroom window, and his fifteen year-old daughter thought she saw someone staring at her when she got out of the shower that morning. Police immediately suspected Allen.

TWENTY

THERE'S AN ITALIAN deli on the north side of Manitowoc called Maretti's. Trays of fresh cold pasta dishes and an assortment of salads are displayed behind glass windows at the counter, and large blocks of Italian and Wisconsin cheeses line the shelves behind. There's a small dining area to the side where comfortable booths surround six or seven tables in the center and hundreds of bottles of wine are neatly arranged in cubby holes along the walls.

Pasta dishes with expertly seasoned Italian meatballs smothered in red tomato sauce, hot or cold subs and sandwiches with generous layers of shaved beef stuffed with green peppers or onions. Or our favorite – thick crust homemade pizza loaded with cheese, sausage, mushrooms, and onions. But it's the atmosphere of the place that keeps us coming back to Maretti's. With a bottle of red Merlot on the table and Frank Sinatra crooning in the background, life is good sitting together in a booth at Maretti's.

I'd spent the last hour at work reading all about Gregory Allen, and I was exhausted from wondering how Kocourek and Vogel could have missed that he was probably Penny Beerntsen's assailant. And having finished another week of running kids all over and helping them with homework, Jody was tired too and in need of a reprieve. So dinner at Maretti's was the perfect antidote for both of us on that first Friday night after the Avery case hit the fan.

But there was no escaping the Avery case. The previous occupants in the booth had left behind that day's edition of the *Journal Sentinel*, and it included another front page article about the exoneration. I picked it up and began skimming it, reading out loud the few parts that we didn't already know about.

The reporter had interviewed Tom Bergner the previous day, and as always Tom was open and honest with what he knew. He said he thought from the start it was probably Allen. In fact, he walked over to the Sheriff's Department a few days after Avery was arrested and told Sheriff Kocourek he thought he might have the wrong guy. He asked Kocourek if he knew how dangerous Allen had recently become, that the police department was even tracking him, but they lost sight of him the afternoon Penny was assaulted. Bergner said he had the impression that the Sheriff knew about Allen's recent conduct, but he told him they'd already ruled him out.

The reporter interviewed Kocourek too, but Kocourek didn't recall having such a conversation with Detective Bergner. He later claimed to investigators from the Attorney General's Office that he wasn't even aware of Allen in 1985, despite the fact that a copy of the criminal complaint charging Allen for the earlier beach incident wasn't only in Vogel's file, it was in the Sheriff's file too.

"Yeah, right," I mumbled to myself.

"What's wrong?" Jody replied.

"Tom Bergner sent me copies of the reports today. There's no way Kocourek didn't know about Allen. This guy's a real piece of work."

I told her how dangerous Allen had become that summer, recounting some of his more bizarre conduct – tapping on windows at three in the morning and then exposing himself to the woman inside, removing screws from windows so he could later break in. I told her about young girls getting out of the shower and seeing eyes peering in at them through the darkness – all the demented, dangerous behavior of a nut case on the loose. Then I told her about the incident just two weeks before he attacked Penny – the night when he broke into a house and tried to assault the girl inside while her parents were up north.

Jody couldn't believe it. "He had a swim suit wrapped around his head?"

"That's right, and he had a knife to her throat."

"Why did he leave?"

"'Cause she told him she was having her period."

"Smart girl."

The pizza came just in time. We were both starving, and at least for awhile we were more interested in the pizza than discussing the Avery case. Between mouthfuls, we looked outside at Buffalo Street and watched some of Manitowoc's nightlife, such as it is. There was an early season chill in the air, but we felt warm and cozy enjoying each other's company in the brightly lit diner with its black and white checkered floor.

I poured us each a second glass of wine, and with Jody patiently putting up with my rambling, I tried to unpeel more layers of what went wrong with Steven Avery's wrongful conviction.

"So why didn't they check out Allen?" Jody asked, resuming our conversation.

"I don't know," I responded, "the Sheriff told Bergner they ruled him out, and Vogel said he had an alibi."

"But he didn't have an alibi," Jody objected.

"I know."

Then I told her that Penny Beerntsen had called the Sheriff and told him a detective from the city police department had called her expressing doubts that they had the right guy.

"What did the Sheriff tell her?"

"Something like, 'Don't listen to the police department, my department has jurisdiction, not the city PD,' you know – that sort of thing."

"Turf war, you mean that's what this was about?" Jody interjected.

"Partly, but it was more than just turf war."

"Like what? What are you suggesting?"

I stared out the window and wondered myself what I was suggesting. In the face of so much doubt, why were Kocourek and Vogel so confident that they had the right guy? After all, more than a dozen witnesses gave police a consistent, detailed account of Avery's whereabouts, and most of them were interviewed within hours of his arrest, so they couldn't have got their stories straight with Avery since he was in isolation at the jail. Their timeline was confirmed by the receipt from Shopko. But none of that mattered – Kocourek and Vogel had their boy, and they plowed full-steam ahead.

In their drive to convict, they ignored any information that ran contrary to Avery's guilt. It meant nothing, for instance, that it took Penny Beerntsen ten minutes to pick out Avery in the live-lineup. And some of the red flags were impossible to miss – like when Penny received the creepy telephone call a few days after the assault, which was consistent with Allen's M.O. when he lunged at the woman on the beach two summers earlier. Both times, he inexplicably knew personal information about his victim.

I'd drifted off in thought, and Jody repeated the question she'd asked me several minutes earlier: "If it wasn't just turf war, then what was it?"

"Avery was on bail for a violent confrontation with a woman who lived down the road from him. He rammed into her car and held her at gunpoint, intending to assault her."

"Did he?"

"No, he let her go – the woman had her baby with her."

"So he was on their radar screen, is that what you're saying?"

"Exactly, and don't forget that his uncle was a deputy sheriff, and the woman he pulled over was married to a deputy too."

"Not real smart – he chooses as his victim a deputy's wife."

"It gets better. The first officer to interview Penny at the hospital that night, her name was Judy Dvorak, she lived across the street from Avery and she knew he was a pervert too. She saw him tether one of his kids to a tree one time. Anyhow, she couldn't stand him. She also knew he was on bail for pulling over the wife of her colleague."

"So, what are you saying? Dvorak just assumed it was Avery because he was a perverted creep and he had another case pending – that doesn't make sense. There are all sorts of sex offenders out there – you guys prosecute them all the time."

"Tell me about it," I replied, "but that's how I think it started. Even though Penny's description of the assailant was generic and didn't match Avery, other than the long hair and the beard, Dvorak just assumed it was him."

Jody cut right to the point: "Well, who matched the victim's description of the assailant better, Avery or Allen?"

"Allen did. Penny said the assailant was short to medium in height, stocky – I think beer belly is the term she used – and that he had brown eyes and long hair with a scraggly beard. Well, Avery's only 5'1'', his eyes aren't brown, they're blue, and believe it or not, he didn't even have a beer belly back then. On the other hand, at 5'10'', brown eyes, with a beer belly, Allen didn't fit the description perfectly, but he fit a lot better than Avery did.

"Okay, so Deputy Dvorak didn't like Avery," Jody replied, "but what about the Sheriff and the other officers who worked the case that night – why were they so certain it was Avery?"

"I don't know, but they jumped right on the bandwagon and then the whole thing took on a life of its own. It's kind of human nature, don't you think? If somebody comes up with a suspect that makes sense, the others are inclined to agree until information arises to the contrary."

"But information did arise to the contrary," Jody replied, "I thought they knew about the alibi the very next day. It sounds like they turned a reasonable suspicion into more than they should have."

She was right. Dvorak and Kocourek reasonably suspected Avery, but a reasonable suspicion is just that – a suspicion. Instead, with absolutely no hard evidence, they drew an unreasonable inference that Avery was the assailant. When they learned information suggesting otherwise, they should have discarded their assumption and started over. But instead, they pressed on, heedless of the consequences. They worked the case in the exact opposite way that police are trained. Instead of gathering and analyzing facts in order to learn the truth, they assumed the truth and then, believing in the rightness of their cause, they adopted the facts that fit their assumption and discarded the rest. This wasn't police work – it was garbage.

I was quiet for awhile, and after I poured myself another glass of wine, for a change it was Jody who broke the silence. "Maybe Vogel and Kocourek felt there was no harm in sending Avery to prison because even though he might not have committed this assault, he was so dangerous that he was bound to commit another."

"Probably, but that's not an excuse. It's rare, but this is a good example of what happens when cops and prosecutors are so convinced that what they're doing is right that they don't care about the constitutional rights of the accused – in fact they're hostile to them. They figure society would be better off with this kind of riffraff behind bars – it's just too bad we have to spend taxpayer money to house them in prison, that's what they think. It's pure arrogance, but that's what it boils down to."

I was good and worked up as we left Maretti's that night. Our conversation had brought the pieces together, and it looked to me like Vogel and Kocourek knew. The identification process at the hospital on the night of the assault was at the very least suggestive, and it might have even been a scam. Once Kusche completed his masterpiece, the dye was cast – a chain of events was set in motion where the machinations of law enforcement took over and their drive to convict never slowed down. Kocourek and Vogel ignored the statements of more than a dozen witnesses that, together with the receipt from the ShopKo store in Green Bay, demonstrated that it was virtually impossible for Avery to commit the crime. And it was hard to imagine how they didn't know it was Allen since the complaint charging him with attempting to commit a nearly identical crime on the same beach where Penny Beerntsen was assaulted was in Vogel's file. A jury convicted the accused, and with the Court of Appeals twice affirming his conviction, an innocent man rotted in prison for eighteen years.

TWENTY-ONE

I PAID LESS attention to the Avery case as the next several months passed by. New challenges replaced old ones at work, and it wasn't long until another Thanksgiving and Christmas were over. The intensity I felt about what happened in 1985 gradually subsided.

But the aftershocks of the wrongful conviction were far from over. Investigators from the Attorney General's Office were hard at work trying to sort out the events that led to Avery's wrongful conviction. They interviewed dozens of witnesses, and in the middle of December, the Attorney General released her report, faxing a copy to our office just minutes before releasing it to the press.

Mark and I read it with great anticipation, wondering what her conclusion would be regarding "what, if any errors occurred during the investigation, and whether any criminal or ethical violations were committed by anyone involved in handling the case," as the report itself described its purpose. Seeing Vogel and Kocourek's shenanigans summarized in one place – in a document authored by the Department of Justice no less – gave the revelations a weight, a substance that they previously lacked. The thirteen-page *Summary of Facts* section was divided into eight sections that detailed conduct by Vogel and Kocourek that I was certain would strike the media and the general public as shocking and inexcusable.

Most of the report covered ground that we were already aware of, but there were a few surprises.

For instance, it turns out that Penny Beerntsen received more than just one disturbing phone call after the assault. Here's the language from the report:

> Penny Beerntsen received harassing phone calls following her assault, even after Steven Avery was arrested. Many of the phone calls were of a sexual nature, some of which occurred five minutes after she would return home, indicating she might be being watched. Such stalking behavior and post-crime contact was consistent with Gregory Allen's past-offense history.

Also, I knew that Vogel's file contained a copy of the police reports and the criminal complaint charging Allen for the beach incident two summers earlier, but the investigators from the AG's office also found copies in the Sheriff's file. In an interview with the *Milwaukee Journal Sentinel* the day after Avery was released from prison, Kocourek claimed he didn't know anything about Allen's crime on the beach two summers earlier, and when the investigators from the AG's office interviewed him, he denied knowing anything about Allen at all. *So what was the complaint doing in his file*, I almost said out loud.

The next revelation was just as disturbing. Shortly after Avery's exoneration, some of our staff told us that they doubted all along that Avery was the assailant, and they thought it was Allen. They approached Denis Vogel and he assured them they had the right guy and that Gregory Allen couldn't have been the assailant because he checked with Allen's probation agent and Allen had an airtight alibi. But the AG's investigators did some checking of their own and found out that Allen wasn't even on probation on the day Penny Beerntsen was attacked. In fact, he wasn't on probation at all during that summer. Vogel, of course, didn't recall having such a conversation with the three members of his staff, even though all three of them independently told the investigators what their boss had said.

But the report's conclusion was hugely disappointing. Given the facts uncovered by the investigators, I thought at the very least the Attorney General would conclude that Vogel and Kocourek had engaged in ethics violations. But she concluded the opposite, and as far as I was concerned, the report was a whitewash.

Her report cited poor communication between law enforcement agencies as one of the primary reasons for the wrongful conviction. But blaming it on poor communication was nonsense. Tom Bergner from the Manitowoc Police Department talked to the Sheriff about Allen, even mentioning that his department was tracking him, and he had the impression that Kocourek already knew. The Two Rivers police report concerning Allen lunging at the woman walking her dog on the same beach two years earlier was even in the Sheriff's file. So how was poor communication among police agencies responsible? It didn't make sense.

Using words without meaning and answering questions by merely restating them, the report opined that "the underlying problem in this case was that the investigators responsible for the investigation into the assault of Ms.

Beerntsen never deemed Allen a suspect." No kidding, I thought to myself. Everyone knew the Sheriff and the DA didn't treat Allen as a suspect – the question was, why not? It was classic bureaucratic doublespeak, and it was hugely disappointing.

It's as if the two investigators wrote the findings of fact, and then some politico wrote the conclusion – the dichotomy was that extreme. The investigators had uncovered egregious facts, but the Attorney General ignored them. She effectively whitewashed the entire affair.

TWENTY-TWO

SNOWBIRDS, THEY CALL them. After the holidays thousands of retirees from Wisconsin flock to the South for the balance of winter – to Florida, to Arizona, to anywhere it's warm. For the rest of us, though, for those who must stay, the exhilaration of last December's snow storms and the excitement of winter's first blast of arctic air have been replaced by the doldrums of mid-winter blues. Cold gray skies alternate with sub-zero temperatures, and, like bears hibernating in their dens, we settle in for the long haul. But lest you end up like Jack Nicholson in *The Shining*, you must occasionally bundle up and get out in the cold. Kids build snow forts or ride sleds and toboggans, some people like snowmobiling, and others go ice fishing. We prefer cross country skiing, and with the right snow conditions, the groomed trails at Point Beach State Park are excellent and it's our favorite place to go.

Our first time out that year was on a Sunday afternoon about a week before Christmas. A winter storm had churned northeast from Oklahoma and having tapped abundant moisture from the Gulf of Mexico along the way, it dumped a foot of snow in the Upper Midwest and left in its wake a Canadian air mass with brilliant sunshine and clear, crisp air. The deep green and brilliant white of the partially snow-covered pine trees contrasted sharply with the clear blue winter sky. Gone were the hustle and bustle of work and the daily concerns of life that fill the minds of parents in their early-forties, and a quiet calm gradually filled our souls.

Three months earlier we had dined at Maretti's and with Steven Avery's wrongful conviction fresh on our minds, our conversation was passionate and intense – fitting for our Italian meal of pizza and wine. I had ranted and raved with a zealot's outrage about the injustice of it all and even questioned what I do for a living. But in the intervening months I had come to accept the wrongful conviction as an aberration that was unlikely to be repeated, thanks in part to the Avery Task Force's anticipated reforms. Besides, we all make mistakes, sometimes even serious ones like Vogel's and Kocourek's, and we wouldn't want others to condemn us if we were in their shoes. It's like a saying I once heard: "There are only two kinds of people: sinners who think they're saints, and saints who know they're sinners."

But then I started backsliding into self-righteousness. The number one duty of a defense attorney is, as the legal ethics code puts it, to "zealously represent" his client. So short of misleading the Court by knowingly participating in a falsehood, the sky is pretty much the limit. But prosecutors are supposed to be different. We're supposed to seek justice, and since the truth is indispensable to justice, we must be firmly grounded in the truth. No doubt, Kocourek and Vogel thought Avery was guilty when they initially charged him, but within a few days they must have known they'd made a mistake. He should have dismissed the charges and started over, but instead, he plowed ahead, like a bull in a china shop.

TWENTY-THREE

L IKE ALL FORMER offenders who have done their time, Steven Avery faced a number of difficult decisions in the days after he was released from prison – some of them more significant than others. Try going out to eat and ordering from the menu when for the last eighteen years you've eaten whatever the prison cooks put on your tray. But there were larger questions too: Where was home, who would he live with, what about work? These are good questions for any former offender as he transitions from prison to life on the outside, and they were especially good questions for someone who went in with deep-seated problems as serious as Steve's.

"Home" turned out to be back at the Avery Salvage Yard with mom and dad. Appearing the day after he was released on a local TV station's nightly news program, Avery was all smiles as he relaxed in his house trailer and popped open a beer. It was the first time I got a good look at him since his release, and by the looks of his girth, the prison food must have agreed with him.

Steven Avery Back at the Auto Salvage

But Steve didn't last long in the house trailer. A person gets accustomed to his surroundings after awhile, and having spent eighteen years in an 8 by 12 foot prison cell, he felt the need for confinement. So that winter he moved into an ice shanty; the close quarters made it feel just like home. "I wanted somethin' small," he told a reporter, "everything was, I don't know, just too big. It didn't feel right."

But it was unlikely he'd live in an ice shanty for long. His lawyers were seeking compensation for what everyone agreed was a horrible injustice, regardless of whether it was by accident or by design, and if Steve played his cards right, before long he'd be a millionaire.

Keith Findley of the Innocence Project led the injustice-by-accident effort by seeking payment from the State Claims Board. Wrongfully convicted persons are permitted under Wisconsin law to petition the State for compensation for the time they spent behind bars. But the law dates back to 1913, and rewards are limited to $5,000 per year, with a cap of $25,000.

So shortly after Steve's release from prison, Findley submitted a massive document entitled "Steven Avery's Petition for Compensation for Wrongful Imprisonment." Not only did he ask the Claims Board to increase the out-of-date limits, but given the egregious circumstances in this case, he suggested that they ignore any limits at all.

He found a receptive audience in the person of Mark Gundrum, the State Assemblyman that Mark and I met in Madison after our visit with the Attorney General. Not a member of the Claims Board itself, but the chair of the Courts and Corrections Committee, Gundrum proposed to raise the limits to $25,000 per year and re-set the cap at $450,000. "I think that's a much more reasonable number," he told the *Milwaukee Journal Sentinel*. "The government has been negligent *per se* in the administration of justice in this case. That's my opinion."

Steve told the press the day he walked out of prison that he wasn't angry with anyone and wasn't really thinking about monetary compensation, but from the looks of the Petition he filed with the Claims Board, he'd obviously changed his mind. Adding only the special damages – loss of income, pension, future earning capacity, those sorts of things – he was seeking an amount "conservatively estimated" at $1,097,200. Steve might not have been thinking money when he got out, but it didn't take long for him to come around.

Even the most fiscally conservative politicians found persuasive the petition's account of the hardships suffered by Steve from spending eighteen years in prison – though I'm sure there was disagreement over the amount of money he requested. Steve was 23 years old and working as an auto mechanic when he was convicted, but now he was 42 years old and was trying hard to overcome the emotional trauma of his wrongful incarceration and to start his life over. He lost his wife and the ability to develop a relationship with his children.

208

"For more than 18 long years," the petition asserted, "Mr. Avery lost his freedom, his civil rights, and his dignity, and through no fault of his own, he was denied the chance to live the American dream – to enjoy the company of his family, to parent his children, to own a home, to advance in a career, and to choose how to live his own life."

The petition went on to describe the immense injuries Steve suffered in terms of "emotional, relational, and personal injuries, social stigma, and the staggering loss of freedom he endured." It tallied economic losses, including 18 years of lost income, social security earnings history, retirement savings, "and more than 18 years in which to acquire skills, increase his level of education, and seize financial and personal opportunities." An actuary put the losses at $1,097,200, and that didn't even include pain and suffering. By granting the request, the petition concluded, the legislature could diminish the "terrible injustice" suffered by Steve and give him "the financial independence with which he may begin his life anew."

* * *

Keith Findley and the Innocence Project staff weren't the only ones seeking compensation for Steven Avery. Despite the ambivalence he initially expressed about bringing a civil action, he soon retained Attorney Walt Kelly and Steve Glynn, the attorney who handled his second appeal, to represent him in a $36,000,000 wrongful conviction lawsuit. That's a lot of zeroes, but how else do you restore someone who lost his freedom for eighteen years? The legal system hasn't figured out a better way than to award them money, and that's exactly what Steve's attorneys set out to accomplish.

Unlike the negligence theory upon which Keith Findley's petition to the Claims Board rested, Kelly and Glynn alleged intent. They filed what lawyers call a 1983 Action, where the plaintiff claims that his or her civil rights were violated – in this case, their client's right to due process under the law. Tom Kocourek and Denis Vogel were named as defendants, both individually and in their official capacities, along with Manitowoc County. In order to succeed, Glynn and Kelly would have to prove the government officials acted intentionally, or at the very least, with gross negligence, when they convicted their client and sent him off to prison.

On a Friday morning, almost a year to the day after Avery was exonerated, Mark and I were both subpoenaed to appear for depositions at the local branch of a large Milwaukee law firm. Walt Kelly would be our inquisitor that day. Whether at trial or in depositions, when it comes to grilling reluctant witnesses, Walt is one of the best. He's an aggressive attorney, but he's not just a hired gun. He passionately believes in his client's cause, and to the extent he pushes the limits of civil advocacy, that's why. His gray beard and piercing blue eyes well-match the personality of this aging but still vibrant activist of the sixties, and although we'd never met, I liked him immediately. Besides, my feelings about what happened back in 1985 weren't a secret. I'd been open with the Department of Justice, and I intended to be the same when I was deposed.

I walked into a conference room where a flock of attorneys looking red-eyed and weary were sitting around a table with pens and legal pads poised in front of them ready to have at their next victim. In addition to Manitowoc County, the lawsuit named Denis Vogel and Tom Kocourek as defendants, both personally and in their official capacities as county employees. Each party had his own attorney, including two each for Vogel and Kocourek, and when I started adding up the legal fees I gave up when I reached over two thousand dollars an hour.

I sat down in the witness chair   the one with the video camera positioned three feet in front of my face – and readied myself for battle. Steven Avery was sitting right beside me, and he appeared to be in good spirits. But who wouldn't be? His case was picking up steam and he was poised to reap millions.

Walt methodically covered the basics first – name, occupation, dates of employment at the DA's office, that sort of thing. Then he zeroed in on what I knew about his client's wrongful conviction. I told him about finding the Gregory Allen complaint in Vogel's file and about my telephone conversation with him a few a few days later. But I couldn't add much to what the lawyers already knew.

I'd been forthcoming with my answers, so when Walt turned me over to the defense, they didn't have much to hone in on and I escaped pretty much unscathed. They'd each received a summary of my interview with the investigators from the AG's Office, they knew where I was coming from, though a few of them seemed none too pleased.

I gathered from one of the attorneys that they were approaching the end of the witness list for depositions and things weren't going well for the County or for its former Sheriff and District Attorney. They'd been zeroing in on Kocourek and Vogel for months, and the two of them were on deck to be deposed. There was little doubt – Steven Avery was about to become a millionaire.

TWENTY-FOUR

PESSIMISM PERMEATES THE trenches of the criminal justice system, and if you thought too much about what happened in the Avery case, it was easy to become discouraged. But Steven Avery's wrongful conviction also brought out the best in people and, as in a surprising number of more ordinary criminal cases, its tragedy was overcome by redemption.

News of his exoneration brought smiles to the faces of those who over the years had believed so firmly in his innocence and fought so tenaciously for his release: Assistant public defender Reesa Evans-Marcinczyk and attorney Jim Bolgert at the trial court level, private investigator James Stefanic, Jack Schairer and then Steve Glynn on appeal, and, of course, Keith Findley and his students at the Innocence Project, who accomplished the ultimate goal – their client's freedom. Some of their efforts fell short, but each of them kept up the drumbeat that Steve was innocent. And for that they had reason to be proud.

The exoneration was especially welcomed news for Jim Bolgert. Steve's conviction wore heavily upon him since the jury handed down the original guilty verdict back in 1985. At times, he testified at his deposition, he felt "grief stricken" over the whole thing. In 2000, he had a conversation with Denis Vogel and told him they had to do something, that it was "a travesty". But when he told Vogel that it was the kind of case that kept him up at night, Vogel replied that it wasn't for him.

For Penny Beerntsen, the emotional aftermath of the exoneration was full of complexity. She is conscientious, maybe to a fault, and compassionate beyond belief, so it wasn't easy for her.

She sent Steve an extraordinary letter a few days after his release from prison. "There are no words sufficient to express how deeply sorry I am for what has happened," she wrote. "Your wrongful conviction has taken away 18 years of your freedom – something that can never be given back to you. I wish it was in my power to restore those years, but it isn't. The only thing I can offer now is a sincere apology that I identified you as my assailant when you were not."

"I work for peace and justice and I feel I'm doing some good, and then I find out that I'm part of a huge miscarriage of justice. When I testified in Court, I honestly believed you were my assailant. I was wrong. I can only say to you, in deepest humility, how profoundly sorry I am. May you be richly blessed, and may each day be a celebration of a new and better life."

And it wasn't just those that were involved in the case who were moved by Steve's exoneration. There was something about his personality and his eighteen years in prison that engendered an extraordinary amount of sympathy for him in the community at large, too. Without sharing any responsibility for his predicament, many felt moved by his plight and reached out to help him in any way they could. After seeing a feature story on TV about his ice shanty abode, a few especially sympathetic souls set up a charity fund for him, and collected close to three thousand dollars from like-minded donors in no time at all.

Attorney General Peg Lautenschlager made the most of it too. By agreeing to conduct an independent review of the wrongful conviction, she had taken on a dicey political endeavor. As the State's "top cop," if she came down too hard on Vogel and Kocourek, she could lose the support of her most natural constituency – law enforcement. Instead, she focused on the positive, even managing to score a few political points along the way.

"DNA evidence has gained acceptance in the criminal justice system as having forceful, potentially irrefutable probative value," she announced in her report. "Had the investigation into the assault of Penny Beerntsen been conducted using currently available technology, it is reasonable to believe that the trial of Steven Avery never would have occurred."

But Steven Avery's exoneration wasn't only followed by a strong emotional response from those who were personally involved and self-congratulations by some of us in government. It also brought reform.

Keith Findley's petition to the state legislature to raise the outdated caps on compensation for wrongfully convicted state prisoners was picking up steam. Governor Jim Doyle advanced the likelihood that the proposal would become law when he enthusiastically endorsed it without passing judgment on the specific amount of money requested by Steve's attorneys.

But the most significant reform would come out of the Avery Task Force.

It hadn't exactly started off with a bang. Politicians were in charge and the media was on hand – always a bad combination for getting anything of substance done. But the hearings were in full swing by the middle of February, and Mark Gundrum and the other members of the Task Force were getting down to business and addressing the issues with the urgency they deserved.

One of the most widely publicized hearings took place at the State Capitol in Madison with both Steven Avery and Penny Beerntsen in attendance. The hearing was held in front of the Judiciary Committee, and many of the heavy hitters in Wisconsin's criminal justice system, along with a few nationally known experts, would be on hand. Wisconsin Supreme Court Justice Louis Butler would address the Committee. So would Chief Deputy Bob Donohoo from the Milwaukee County DA's office, nationally known DNA guru Norm Gahn, and several state senators and circuit court judges with an abiding interest in criminal justice system reform.

The hearing would focus on the perils of eyewitness identification, but it was clear from the agenda that other issues would also be confronted. In fact, one of the main things to come out of the Task Force – a requirement that police officers either audio or videotape interrogations of juvenile suspects and a strong incentive that they do the same with adults – had nothing at all to do with Steven Avery's wrongful conviction.

But the most anticipated testimony would come from Penny Beerntsen. Here's how *Milwaukee Journal Sentinel* reporter Tom Kertscher covered that part of the story:

> The sexual assault victim who falsely identified Steven Avery as her attacker, helping send him to prison for more than seventeen years, is to appear Tuesday at the Capitol before a task force. The Manitowoc woman plans to cite a lack of "moral

courage" on the part of top Manitowoc County officials who investigated the 1985 assault. She plans to blame law enforcement authorities for not telling her that Gregory A. Allen – whom DNA testing linked to her attack in September – had been identified, with Avery, as a suspect.

The woman, 55, is to urge the task force to review ... the need for investigators 'to commit to writing discussions about other potential suspects'.

She also plans to tell about the guilt she has experienced since Avery was exonerated five months ago. 'Of all the people I need to learn to forgive in this whole process, forgiving myself will be the most difficult,' the woman says in a statement she plans to make in Madison. 'Not a day goes by that I don't think about Mr. Avery, his family and the suffering they endured.'

The hearing was held two days later, and in a dramatic moment for all those who witnessed it, Penny Beerntsen embraced Steve and asked him for forgiveness. She later described his response – that she needn't worry and that it wasn't her fault – as "probably one of the most grace-filled things ever said to me."

Longtime *Milwaukee Journal Sentinel* columnist Bill Janz covered the story. He noted Penny's restorative justice work in the prisons and described how inmates admire her courage and appreciate her efforts to help them. Some of them had recently written to her and defended her in the assault case, "as she has defended them as human beings, not monsters," Janz wrote.

TWENTY-FIVE

MY SONS AND I go salmon fishing at the end of every summer – how often depends on how they're biting that year. Running from mid-August through late September, the salmon run is a blast. Chinook, or sometimes called "King" Salmon aren't native to Lake Michigan – the Department of Natural Resources stocked them thirty years ago. Bellies bulging with eggs, the twenty pound behemoths stage just offshore before swimming up-river to spawn. Charter boats take well-heeled tourists from Milwaukee and Chicago into the deeper waters all summer long. But when the spawn is on, in August and September, local anglers like us along with some diehard pier fishermen from Minnesota and Iowa, take part in the fun.

We went out on the last Saturday in September that year, the day after I was deposed in Steven Avery's lawsuit, and after stopping for a healthy breakfast at Kwik Trip – soda and candy bars for the boys, and coffee and donuts for me – we were at the Two Rivers pier by quarter to six. Two or three more serious fishermen beat us to the most coveted spots at the end of the pier, but there was plenty of room, so I set up about thirty yards beyond the boys and started casting. Green and silver three-quarter ounce Champs are the standard fishing lure during the spawn, but anything that makes them angry will do. Not particularly caring if anything with gills struck my lure, but hoping I could at least avoid a snag by staying off the bottom, I casted over the water and watched the Champ arc far over the waves.

It was warm for that time of year – felt more like August than the end of September – and a late summer thunderstorm had passed through an hour earlier, leaving dark scraggly clouds in its wake as it moved out to sea. The sky turned from pink to red and then to purple as the sun rose triumphantly over the departing storm.

I was happily lost in a fisherman's reverie with my thoughts drifting off in all manner of direction – until they settled on the Avery case. Maybe it was because I'd seen him just the day before while being deposed, but whatever the reason, the events surrounding his wrongful conviction were once again on my mind.

Like the storm's high winds that downed trees and knocked out power lines a few hours earlier, Kocourek and Vogel's actions had severely damaged the local justice system. The media had forever linked Manitowoc County with Steven Avery – the innocent man who spent eighteen years in prison for a crime he didn't commit. And if that wasn't enough, local citizens who already mistrusted the police distrusted them even more, and those who did trust them started to wonder why.

But now the storm was over. Avery's exoneration had overcome the injustice of his wrongful conviction, and like the dark clouds drifting out to sea in front of me, the turmoil wrought by the Avery case was slowly receding. Smart lawyers and committed government officials were trying to restore his life to what it was before, or at least to salve the injury with a boatload of money, and to prevent something similar from happening again. They were working hard to repair the damage, and a measure of justice was being restored.

I like severe summer thunderstorms, and while I prefer to experience them myself I also like hearing about close encounters of others. So even though I wasn't here to see it, the storm that struck Manitowoc in the summer of 1950 intrigued me the first time I heard about it, and now, as the circumstances surrounding Avery's wrongful conviction continued to unfold, my thoughts turned to that horrible storm.

Attorney Ron Kaminski, who made a brief appearance as a special prosecutor in the Avery saga after Dennis Vogel left for greener pastures, first told me about the storm. He described how natural light filtered in through the glass panes of the dome during the day and artificial light shined forth at night – displacing the darkness, like light from a cathedral. Then on June 28, 1950, a terrific hailstorm swept through the city and obliterated the dome. By replacing the glass with steel, construction workers did their best to restore the dome, but eventually even steel corrodes, and after a few decades the Courthouse dome came to look unsightly.

There was no way of knowing it then, but the efforts to compensate Steven Avery and to restore a measure of justice to the court system would fall short too. The original injustice was about to explode. The first storm was about to spawn a second one, a storm so powerful that it would shatter the atmosphere and lay waste to parts of the land.

.

Part III

TWENTY-SIX

O N HALLOWEEN DAY 2005, twenty-five year-old freelance photographer Teresa Halbach hopped in her blue Toyota RAV4 and drove to the Avery Auto Salvage. Teresa worked for Pearce Photography in Green Bay, and one of her accounts was with Auto Trader Magazine, a company that listed vehicles for sale in classified ads. Her last assignment that day was to snap a few pictures of a maroon Plymouth Voyager that Steven Avery was putting up for sale.

Teresa graduated with honors from the University of Wisconsin-Green Bay where she majored in photography. She specialized in taking portraits of children, but she also took wedding pictures for friends. Her brother Mike later told a reporter that she had a gift for making people feel comfortable, and it showed in her photography.

She grew up in the village of St. John in Calumet County, one county west of Manitowoc, where her parents ran a dairy farm. She had been living in Green Bay, but recently decided to pursue her dream of opening her own studio, so to help make ends meet, she and a friend moved back to a house on her parent's property.

Teresa had been at the Avery Salvage Yard several times before and except for the last time, her assignments had been uneventful. On her last visit, Steve had come out of the shower wrapped only in a towel, and although she was a little unnerved by the incident, mentioning it to a close friend, with all the publicity about Steve's exoneration and the sympathy poured for him by so many in the community, she may not have thought much of it. Besides, every other assignment had gone off without a hitch.

Teresa loved singing along with just about anything on the radio and she may have been singing along as she drove east down Highway 10 toward the Avery Salvage Yard. She especially loved karaoke. A friend said later that when it was her turn to take to the stage, Teresa became the life of the party.

Teresa's mother started worrying when she hadn't heard from her daughter in three days – she was never out of touch that long. So she called the police and reported her missing.

Teresa Halbach

* * *

After forty hours of scraping and painting someone else's house, the last thing a professional painter wants to do is to scrape and paint his own. It's the same with prosecutors. We deal with enough of society's ills during the day that we don't need to read more about them at night. So like most of my colleagues, I don't pay much attention to crime in the rest of the state, or in the rest of the country for that matter. The nation's obsession with JonBenét Ramsey's disappearance, for instance, wasn't my obsession. Of course the OJ case was an exception, but everyone who was vertical got into that one.

So I missed it when news first broke that Teresa Halbach had gone missing. But my ignorance about her disappearance didn't last long. Mark called me at home on Saturday morning, and from the tone of his voice I knew it was serious. Could I meet him out at the Avery Salvage Yard, he asked – right away. A volunteer search party had just found the SUV of a young woman from Calumet County who was reported missing three days earlier, and the police needed a search warrant for what they feared would be her remains.

"Where'd they find the SUV?" I asked.

"At the edge of the junkyard near the woods, whoever did it threw a bunch of branches on top to conceal it."

"Do we know anything else yet?"

"Well," Mark replied, "her final shot that day was of a used car for sale at the Salvage Yard. And guess who called to set up the appointment?"

"Oh shit," I replied.

Mark was right. It proved to be Teresa's final shot all right, for she never left the Avery Salvage Yard that day – at least not in one piece. She was tied up, raped, knifed, and shot to death – and then cut into pieces and burned.

223

I hopped in our van and sped out to the Salvage Yard. Media helicopters circled overhead as nearly two hundred police officers from three different counties and the State Patrol conducted a massive search for what everyone feared would be Teresa's body. I remember gathering information from detectives for a search warrant and wondering where in the midst of the countless skeletons of junked cars, each surrounded by tall grass and weeds, the killer had hidden the body. As darkness fell, a light drizzle that started in mid-afternoon turned into a cold driving rain. A mobile unit from the State Crime Lab with a couple flood lights and a space heater served as the command post and a refuge from the dark and the wet and the cold. The rain got heavier as the night wore on, and the flimsy transparent plastic that served as the canopy for the crime lab unit flapped noisily in the gusty wind. I'll never forget the eerie feeling evoked by the shrill sound of police dogs loudly barking as the search continued late into the night. Still no body ... until finally one of the dogs hit on a fire pit containing tooth fragments and bones that a forensic anthropologist later identified as belonging to an adult human female.

Steve Glynn and Walt Kelly got word the next morning. The local television stations had blitzed the story on the previous evening's news, and by the following morning it was the lead story in newspapers and electronic media across the entire State. Glynn tried desperately to get a hold of his client, but Steve was up north at his parents' cabin. Steve Glynn is a calm and thoughtful man who cares deeply about his clients, regardless of how despicable the crime is they are suspected of committing, so I'm sure he approached Steve gingerly. But about one matter, he had to be direct: under no circumstances, he advised his client, was he to talk about the incident – not to the media, and not to police. '

But Steve ignored him on both counts and blabbed freely to anyone with a microphone or a pen. Thanks to the attention lavished upon him two years earlier, he wasn't a bit shy of the cameras and he enjoyed being in front of the klieg lights again. He granted interviews with several newspapers and television reporters from his family cabin up north and told them he had nothing to do with Teresa Halbach's murder.

He conceded that Teresa was at the Salvage Yard that day. She was there to take pictures of a minivan for a classified ad he was placing in Auto Trader Magazine. She'd been there several times before taking pictures of other vehicles and that's all she was doing on the day she disappeared. Steve said he remembered seeing a pickup truck that he'd never seen in the area before pull up right behind Teresa as she pulled off of Avery Road and headed back to the main highway a little after two p.m. In response to one reporter's question about how Teresa's RAV4 ended up on his family's land, he said he was worried the police might be trying to set him up again – just like the last time. Maybe the Manitowoc County cops planted it, he said.

Two nights later, 250 people held a candlelight vigil in hopes of Teresa's safe return. Although the authorities and the rest of the public assumed the charred bones and teeth fragments found in the fire pit belonged to Teresa, DNA tests were still under way, so there was nothing definitive. They held a prayer service and tied blue ribbons on trees, at first as a sign of hope that Teresa would come home, but later as kind of a remembrance. The ribbons were blue in honor of Teresa's favorite color.

Teresa's brother, Mike Halbach, worked as a video assistant for the Green Bay Packers, and he would serve as the Halbach family's spokesperson throughout the entire ordeal.

Trying hard to remain hopeful, Mike spoke to a reporter after the vigil.

"We hope Teresa will come home, but we don't know where she is," he said calmly, "but at the same time we are preparing for the worst. Until we know where she is, we definitely think she'll come home to us."

But Teresa never did come home. A few days later, DNA tests confirmed what everyone suspected all along: the tooth fragments and bones in the fire pit next to Steven Avery's trailer were Teresa's.

Mike Halbach spoke to the media again after receiving the news: "It hurts to know that we won't see Teresa on Earth, you know, as far as we know, but we'll move on. It will take awhile to move on, but we'll see Teresa again."

Candlelight vigil for Teresa

TWENTY-SEVEN

ALTHOUGH THEY DENIED it, from the moment police got word that Teresa Halbach's vehicle had been found at the Avery Salvage Yard, they considered Steven Avery to be the number one suspect for her murder. And like it was the last time they investigated him for a serious crime, at least in the beginning, their suspicion was a reasonable one. He was the last person known to have seen Teresa alive and her car was concealed on his property, and when he called her employer that morning to set up an appointment, he specifically asked for her and not some other girl.

News of Teresa's disappearance had already garnered some national media attention, but when it became known that the man suspected of killing her had spent eighteen years in prison for a crime he didn't commit, the story took off like thunder. It was, and still is, the only time in the nation's history when an exonerated person was later arrested for murder, and the *Deliverance*-like crime scene and grisly details of the murder guaranteed it a national audience.

In what must be one of the show's strangest episodes ever, Steven Avery called into of the *Nancy Grace* show on CNN a few days after the human remains in the fire pit were identified as belonging to Teresa Halbach. Still holed up at the family cabin up north, he again proclaimed his innocence, telling America that he was being set up by the Manitowoc County Sheriff's Department in revenge for his $36 million lawsuit.

"Mr. Avery," Nancy Grace asked, "Why do you feel that you're being framed?"

"Because every time I turn around, the County's out here doing something to me."

When asked about the tooth fragments and bones that were found in his fire pit, Steve said the Salvage Yard isn't usually locked and anyone could just drive right in.

"I worry about it every minute," he said. "I look out the window, is a squad car here, are they going to pick me up? When are they going to pick me up? When I'm sleeping, are they going to come in? I always have that fear."

"I think Manitowoc County is trying to set me up real good because they're taking everything," he said, "but they don't seem like they found anything because there ain't nothing there. They've been watching us. They've been sitting up by the end of the driveway. But I'm done talking to them."

Calumet County District Attorney Ken Kratz charged Steve two days later with first degree intentional homicide and mutilation of a corpse. Kratz was appointed special prosecutor after Mark Rohrer – citing a conflict of interest because of Avery's pending lawsuit against the County, including its former DA – bowed out. Ken's a very good prosecutor, but he loves the limelight, so he was more than happy to prosecute the case. Also, Teresa was from Calumet County and Ken had been working with his Sheriff's department since the investigation into her disappearance began.

Dressed in a black and white striped jail jumpsuit, with his wrists handcuffed and attached to a belly belt, Steve was escorted into Court by eight uniformed deputies. Judge Patrick Willis set $500,000 cash bail. In a strange bit of irony, his arrest occurred on the same day the Governor was scheduled to sign into law the "Avery Bill" in the same courtroom where he was wrongfully convicted twenty years earlier. But with news of the Bill's namesake's arrest, the ceremony was promptly called off and the legislation was rather blandly renamed the "Criminal Justice Reforms Package."

Self-serving proclamations of innocence or not, somewhere along the line, the innocent man had turned into a cold-blooded killer. Or had he?

Steven Avery escorted to court

TWENTY-EIGHT

S OMEBODY MENTIONED AT work the next day that *Nancy Grace* was supposed to cover the Avery case again that night, so I made sure to tune in. Sitting in for Nancy, guest host Harris Faulkner opened the show with a video clip of a somber looking Ken Kratz conducting another press conference.

"It's no longer a question, at least in my mind, of who is responsible for the death of Teresa Halbach," he said, pushing well beyond the limits of what prosecutors are supposed to say to the media. Trying to deflect any left-over sympathy for Avery from those who couldn't accept that "the innocent man" could have committed such a heinous crime, Kratz reminded the viewers that there was one victim in the case – and that was Teresa Halbach.

Faulkner turned to former prosecutor Wendy Murphy after a commercial break – presumably for her expertise.

"Wendy," he asked, "If you're prosecuting this case, what does all this evidence tell you?"

"Well, this doesn't take rocket science," the former prosecutor began. "It doesn't get any closer to a slam dunk, even without knowing yet that it is, in fact, this woman."

Apparently, facts didn't matter to Wendy Murphy.

"I mean, I've got to tell you something," she said with disgust in her voice, "the sympathy for this guy, the idea that he's filed this lawsuit, I just want to reach through this camera and grab the guy and shake him and bang his head on the wall because I'm not convinced at all that he was wrongly convicted of the first crime!"

"I will not deny for a minute that the DNA evidence that wasn't available at the time of his trial kind of affected his ability to have a fair trial," she continued. "But let's not confuse this with innocence. I'm not persuaded at all that this guy was innocent with regard to that earlier rape!"

"So let me say this to the people who helped him get out. Good job! You let the guy out by claiming he's innocent. "And now look what he did. He killed a woman! Thanks a lot!"

"But he was exonerated," Faulkner interjected.

"That doesn't mean he's innocent," she snapped back. "I'm sick of these DNA lies. The Innocence Project and these people who falsely claim that 150 men have been exonerated and proved actually innocent with these new DNA tests on old cases is nonsense."

"I don't care how many shows he goes on and claims he's not the type of guy that does this sort of thing," she continued. "How does he explain the bucket of blood from his body in her car?"

"'Bucket of blood' -- what's she talking about," I said out loud, "I thought it was a few stains."

Next, they brought in a forensic psychologist who opined the obvious – that whoever committed the murder was "a stone-cold sociopath."

"To put a dead body in a barrel," the expert said, "to light it on fire, the sights, the smells, the sounds, to watch it burn. That says that this is a man who has no care for human life."

No kidding.

Locally, Steven Avery's arrest for Teresa's murder wasn't just a bizarre news story that would capture national attention for a week before Nancy Grace and others in the media moved on to some other salacious crime story. It was the talk of the town, and sometimes in the entire state, and it would remain so for months, if not years, ahead.

Everybody, of course, was shocked by the news. Some people couldn't bring themselves to believe that their former hero was actually a monster. Why would he ruin his life by murdering Teresa Halbach? He was about to become a millionaire – there's no way he would do such a thing! But a majority assumed he was guilty – why would the police have arrested him if he wasn't involved?

Being a prosecutor, I thought he was guilty too. I'd seen it happen before, how an offender can swing from trying his hardest to stay on the straight and narrow one day to committing a horribly violent crime on the next. And given my prior obsession with Avery's wrongful conviction, I was more familiar than most with his sordid past, going all the way back to when he was a juvenile.

But on the other hand, I had personal contact with him on two separate occasions during the month before Teresa was murdered, and in neither instance did it seem like he was about to commit such a heinous crime.

The first time I saw him was in connection with the arrest of his then-newfound girlfriend, Carla Schwartz, for drunken driving. The case came up for trial almost a year after the incident, and Steve was the star witness for the defense.

Carla had put her car in the ditch out on Reifs Mills Road. She crawled out of the car after the crash and walked up to a nearby farmhouse to call a friend for a ride home, but when they pulled into Carla's driveway, a County Sheriff's deputy was patiently awaiting her arrival. Carla started crying. "Yes, I was driving," she told the officer, "I was alone at the time." She said she got into an argument with her boyfriend and she was driving around to clear her head. "I went in the ditch because it was so damn foggy," she blurted out.

It was the fifth time she'd been busted for drunk driving, which even in Wisconsin is a felony, and she had six other criminal convictions on her record too – disorderly conduct, resisting an officer, misdemeanor theft, and other similar petty offenses. Her blood alcohol concentration this time was a healthy .285 – more than three times the legal limit – and it was the drunken driving charge that would net her the most time.

I knew the case was coming up on my trial calendar, but I hadn't given it much thought until I received a letter from Steven Avery. The letter was hand-written and it wasn't easy to read, but the gist of it was that Carla didn't put the car in the ditch; he did. If the cops would just do their job and investigate, Steve wrote, they'd know what happened and he and his sweetheart wouldn't be in such a pickle. He said he didn't want to get involved, but he couldn't take Carla being in jail anymore – he loved her and wanted to marry her.

The day for trial arrived and there was Steve, in the same courtroom where Judge Hazlewood sentenced him nearly twenty years earlier. We'd never met, but I knew what he looked like and I think he knew who I was too. His girlfriend's attorney and I exchanged a few pleasantries and then the Judge called in the jury.

Steve told the same tall tale at trial as he did in his letter. He and Carla met each other for the very first time at the Uni-Mart out on Highway R that night, and after some small talk, Carla asked him to go for a ride. He said he didn't have anything else to do that night, so he took her up on the offer. Even though it was Carla's car, he drove. He told the jury they aimlessly drove around the County for awhile, and then Carla asked if he could take her out to the Salvage Yard to show her around. A junked vehicle was blocking the entrance, so he used Carla's car to push it away, but he hit the gas too hard and the car slipped off the bumper and rammed into the front end of the junked car. With Carla's car still drivable, Steve continued, they went for another ride, but then the fog rolled in, and after missing a turn he put Carla's car in the ditch. He said he called his sister to come get them, but Carla said she was going home and she started walking the other way.

But his story wasn't believable, and the jury didn't buy it. Carla told the arresting officer several times that she was the driver, and she never said a word about anyone else being with her. So she was convicted, and a few months later Judge Hazlewood placed her on probation and gave her nine months in the county jail.

Steve and I crossed paths again a few weeks later, this time when I was deposed in his 36 million dollar lawsuit against the County. He was seated right next to me and we nodded to each other when I walked in and did the same when I left. Without saying it out loud, the message from each of us was that there were no hard feelings. Steve sat politely and listened attentively as the lawyers asked their questions and I did my best to answer.

There was nothing about his appearance on either occasion to suggest that his sexual deviance – which was so evident when he was younger – was about to explode. On the contrary, his demeanor both times was non-threatening and calm, even friendly, I'd say.

TWENTY-NINE

THE MANITOWOC COUNTY Circuit Court operates under a monthly intake cycle. Whether it's civil or criminal, traffic or juvenile, or any other type of dispute that can be settled in a court of law, if you're the Intake Judge, it's yours. You'll start it, and you'll see it through to the end.

Judge Patrick Willis was on Intake when the Avery murder charges were filed. Since assuming the bench seven years earlier, he had drawn more than his fair share of high-profile trials, and by good luck or ill, he now drew the Avery trial, the most sensational trial in the County's history – hands down.

The case passed predictably enough through the usual mile-markers of the criminal justice system with the press covering each hearing more than its significance deserved. The Initial Appearance, the Preliminary Examination, the Arraignment – front page headlines and nightly news reports covered each of them to satisfy the public's appetite for the latest news.

In the months leading up to trial, the parties filed every motion under the sun and, as always, Judge Willis dug in and rose to the challenge. Some of the motions had more merit than others, but he plowed through them one at a time and methodically disposed of each, according to law.

* * *

Having already invested hundreds of pricey hours in a civil lawsuit that had abruptly lost most of its value, neither Steve Glynn nor Walt Kelly were inclined to defend Steve against the murder charges. Besides, there was probably a conflict of interest. So Assistant Public Defender Erik Loy was appointed instead. Like Glynn and Kelly before him, Loy tried gagging his client, but true to form, Steve ignored him and granted one interview after another from the Calumet County jail, claiming more boldly each time that he was being set up by the police.

"Whoever killed Teresa Halbach ain't got a right mind," he told one reporter. "There's no way I could kill somebody – that would be too hard."

"They know what to look for," he said, referring to the police, "so they know what they should plant and where they should plant it."

In an interview with the same reporter, Delores Avery, Steve's mother, backed up his claim: "I don't know why the hell they do that stuff. They must like wrecking people's lives."

"He's innocent, I know it in my heart," she said, describing how people in the grocery store and on the streets were looking at her again.

Steve's dad, Allan Avery, told the reporter that the cops were wrong before and now they're wrong again. "Now it's starting all over again," he said, gazing out at his salvage yard.

Kratz responded, telling reporters that Steve and his family's allegations of planting evidence were "absurd." He said someone would need a vial of Steve's perspiration to plant his DNA on Teresa's car keys. As it turned out, Ken's choice of the word "vial" turned out to be an unwise one.

Steve Glynn and Walt Kelly were deeply disappointed when the investigation into Teresa Halbach's murder increasingly pointed in their client's direction. "This case has blown us away," Glynn told a reporter from the *Journal Sentinel*. "I haven't taken that hard a punch in a long, long time."

"This lets down so many people," he went on. "It became something that could have had an enormously positive effect on the criminal justice system in this state, but now that's up in the air."

News of Avery's likely involvement wasn't easy for Keith Findley either. The Wisconsin Innocence Project's brochure described its mission as not just to release the innocent, but also to find the truth and properly punish those truly responsible for crimes. "This is a very emotional time and a very emotional event," Findley said to a reporter. "But this should not affect what we do."

The Innocence Project has steadfastly continued its work, winning the release of additional wrongfully convicted inmates along the way. But not without cost: in the weeks immediately following Teresa Halbach's murder, Keith Findley and his family received death threats in connection with Steven Avery's release from prison two years before Teresa was murdered.

* * *

With twenty-five years of experience under his belt and the typical heart of a public defender, Erik Loy is an excellent attorney. But like so many criminal defendants ignorantly say when they decline the free services of the public defender, Steve wanted "a real lawyer" instead. So he turned to the big leagues. He promptly settled his lawsuit for a fraction of its worth – $400,000, to be precise – and retained a talented but pricy legal defense team from Madison and Milwaukee. In a classic good cop/bad cop routine, Dean Strang of Madison and Jerome Buting of Milwaukee would tag-team the prosecution from the day they were hired until the end of the trial.

Responding to Kratz' frequent and sometimes over-the-top interviews with the media, and aware themselves that nearly everyone in the state had its attention glued to the case, Buting and Strang tried much of their case in the press. They methodically shot down the State's key pieces of evidence one at a time and then leaked a bombshell or two of their own.

They started dribbling out a few weeks after Steve was arrested – a series of quirky circumstances – coincidences, I thought at the time – that made some people start to wonder whether the police could have done it again.

Exhibit A was the RAV4. Investigators from the Calumet County Sheriff's Department learned early on that Steve was the last person known to have seen Teresa Halbach alive, so it made sense that they began their search at the Avery Salvage Yard. But when they searched the property, they found nothing. The RAV4 wasn't found until four days later by the volunteer search party organized by her family and friends. The Salvage Yard stretches over forty acres of grassy hills and is littered with more than a thousand skeletons of junked cars, so many people assumed that either Steve moved it, or the police just missed it. But others weren't so sure.

Buting and Strang masterfully seized upon the circumstances of the RAV4's delayed discovery. Calumet

County officers didn't find it because it wasn't there – it must have been planted. The police didn't murder Teresa Halbach, they'd never do such a thing, but Manitowoc County deputies probably found her car somewhere nearby after she was reported missing and then drove it to the Salvage Yard to make it look like Steve killed her. It was all part of the effort to frame their client and wrongfully convict him again. Their motive: revenge for Steve's thirty-six million dollar lawsuit against the County that made the Sheriff's Department look bad.

The second shoe dropped a few weeks later. It had to do with how Teresa's keys, including the ignition key to her RAV4, were found. Among the locations the police searched on the first night of their investigation was Steve's bedroom. The initial searches of the room conducted by Calumet County officers yielded nothing – they were looking for more direct evidence at that time – like blood or other clues as to what happened to Teresa.

But a few days later, two Manitowoc County Sheriff's Department officers, Detective Jim Lenk and Sergeant Andy Colborn, searched the bedroom again. It was the third time the room was searched, but they wanted to check behind a bookcase. They moved it away from the wall and a set of keys fell out, landing on the floor right in front of them. They were Teresa's keys and one of them, the key to the RAV4, was later discovered to contain some skin cells that matched Steven Avery's DNA.

I knew Lenk and Colborn. They're two of the most honest and ethical cops I've ever worked with, and I knew in my heart and my mind that they'd be the last ones in the world to plant evidence. I didn't know why the other officers missed the keys on the previous searches, but I assumed I'd find out soon enough.

But Buting and Strang cried foul. Lenk and Colborn had both been deposed in Steve's wrongful conviction lawsuit just a few weeks before Teresa disappeared, and Steve's lawyers had roughed them up pretty good. They grilled them, focusing upon whether they knew if Sheriff Kocourek was aware that Steve might have been innocent of assaulting Penny Beerntsen, and that the real assailant was somebody else.

But it wasn't just the timing of their depositions – it was also the subject matter. About ten years after Steve was wrongfully convicted, Colborn received a telephone call from a detective in Green Bay. An inmate in the Brown County Jail was claiming that another man was serving time in prison for a sexual assault that he, the inmate, committed about ten years earlier on a beach in Manitowoc County. Colborn never got the inmate's name, but Gregory Allen was incarcerated at the Brown County Jail at the time of the call. Colborn told Lenk and they sent a message up the chain of command, but they were told to stay out of it, that they already had the right guy.

The whole subject was uncomfortable for both of them, and they didn't appreciate being dragged into the middle of it by Avery's attorneys. It seemed like a tremendous stretch to me, but Buting and Strang claimed they were angry and embarrassed about the allegations against their department and implied that was their motive for planting the key.

Neither Colborn nor Lenk had anything to do with Steven Avery's wrongful conviction – they weren't even involved in the investigation. But still, the coincidence seemed awfully strange, and before long the number of people who suspected the police set up Avery again rose sharply.

* * *

The news got even worse a few months later – much worse. In one of the most dramatic turn of events since Teresa

Halbach went missing, Jerome Buting called a press conference that shocked the state and propelled the case back in front of the national spotlight. By the time it was over, the defense had stolen the ball and pushed it up court so explosively that the prosecution of Steven Avery for Teresa's murder was in serious jeopardy.

Ostensibly as part of his trial prep, but in fact purely fishing, Buting had requested several months earlier to see the court file from the wrongful conviction back in 1985. It was the same file – actually a box full of court records and exhibits – that the deputy clerk had found in the courthouse basement during Avery's second appeal ten years earlier. Buting walked into the Clerk's office at the appointed time and saw the file just sitting there, unattended on the counter. He rifled through the box and quickly came upon an unsealed vial of his client's blood. It was the blood specimen Sherry Culhane used to compare Steve's DNA to the fingernail scrapings taken from Penny Beerntsen on the night of her assault back in 1985.

A few splotches of Steve's blood had been found in Teresa's car, and now the defense had an explanation for how they got there. It was the cops! They must have secreted some of his blood from the vial in the Clerk's office and spattered a few drops in Teresa's car. With fake disgust, Buting described to the media how the box was just sitting there, unattended on the counter, available for anyone with the inclination to pilfer through at will.

But if you're going to allege a police conspiracy, it better be credible – though it helps if the alleged conspirators had previously conspired. So how did the police get their hands on the blood specimen? For Buting and Strang, it was easy. The courthouse bailiffs are employed by the Sheriff's Department. They have keys to the Clerk's office, and thereby access to the vial. They could have snuck in after hours and retrieved some blood from the vial and then handed it off to one of the detectives, who could have sped out to the Salvage Yard and placed a drop or two in Teresa's car.

Either Buting had stumbled upon the mother of all red herrings, or there was something to the conspiracy theory.

I thought it couldn't get any worse, but a few months later the defense filed a *Denny* motion, named after the Wisconsin Supreme Court case of the same name. They wanted the Judge to allow them to present evidence to the jury that some specific person or persons other than the defendant might have murdered Teresa Halbach.

And their Motion carried some weight. Steve wasn't the only member of the Avery clan to have had trouble with the law. His older brother Chuck had a violent past, most notably an incident in 1999 when his former wife accused him of sexual assault and attempting to strangle her with a telephone cord. His younger brother Earl had potential too. He pleaded no contest to battery and sexual assault charges in 1992, stemming from an attack on his current wife. And both of them had "opportunity" since they worked at the Avery Auto Salvage and would have been in the area when Teresa was murdered.

The situation had me on edge. It was bad enough that the Calumet County investigators didn't find Teresa's RAV4 when they initially searched the Salvage Yard and that Colborn and Lenk were the ones to find her keys in Steve's bedroom. But now, with the sensational blood vial defense, and the defense pointing fingers at two other members of the Avery clan who sounded at least as screwed up as Steve, there was a legitimate shot that he could go free.

THIRTY

Half a block from the Courthouse, right downtown, Warren's Restaurant has been the pulse of the community in Manitowoc for almost fifty years. It's one of those greasy spoons that grace most every American small town. With bottomless cups of coffee and a menu of breakfast items that are more than just passable, it's an early morning gathering spot for local lawyers and anyone else who enjoys shooting the bull. Local, state, national, or beyond – there's no problem too large or too small for the folks at Warren's to solve. Mostly, though, it's a place of friendship and fellowship where just like at *Cheers*, everyone knows your name.

As a morning person and a hopeless coffee addict committed to non-recovery, I'm one of the regulars at Warren's, or at least a semi-regular, stopping in a few mornings every week. It opens at six and I like to get there around 6:30 to join the earliest of the early morning crowd.

The Avery case was naturally the chief topic of discussion at Warrens from the date of Teresa Halbach's disappearance until the end of the trial. From Mike the window washer to the county executive, everyone at Warrens had an opinion about the case, and given what I do for a living, they inevitably asked about mine.

For the most part their opinions didn't evolve. Some thought from the start that Avery was guilty as sin, that the conspiracy theory was nothing but a pack of lies spewed out by a couple high priced out of-town defense attorneys. And their opinions didn't change when Lenk and Colborn found the key – just more conspiracy theory nonsense as far as they were concerned. Take Joe, for instance – every time I'd walk by, he'd shake an imaginary blood vial and ask me if I'd been out at the Salvage Yard with the coppers lately. What a card.

Tammy, on the other hand, was the complete opposite. She bought the defense wholeheartedly. Of course the cops set him up – every one of them is a lying stinking bum. Just last month they nailed her teenage son for writing another forged check, and this time he didn't even do it – he only took the plea bargain to avoid going to jail. She was absolutely convinced that the conspiracy theory was true.

* * *

The defense team had been suspiciously quiet. The conspiracy theory was the cornerstone of their defense, but they hadn't filled in the blanks yet. Any day, I feared, they'd start leaking the embarrassing, no, the inexcusable details surrounding the defendant's wrongful conviction twenty years earlier, and the public would be shocked all over again – this time by the conduct of the police. I dreaded how effectively they would manipulate those events and tie them to the murder charges.

245

Transforming a juror's anger against an accused murderer to sympathy for him instead wouldn't be easy, but if anybody could pull it off, it would be Buting and Strang. If the jury became mired in the details of the wrongful conviction, who knows what would happen. All it would take is one out of twelve, one conspiracy-minded juror who thought like half the folks at Warren's did, and Steven Avery would go free. Forget about convicting him – by the time the defense was finished spinning their tale, the jury would be ready to hang the prosecution instead.

But maybe my fear was misplaced. Maybe I was attaching more significance to the details surrounding the wrongful conviction than they deserved. I'd been consumed by those events for a long time, but whether they were relevant to the murder charges and thereby admissible at trial, was far from certain. I knew that sooner or later the parties would have to address the issue head on, and Judge Willis would have to decide.

I tried to take comfort in the fact that the law was on our side on this one, and when it comes to rationally and objectively applying the law to the facts at hand, Judge Willis is one of the best.

The rule is straightforward enough: relevant evidence is generally admissible, but if the probative value of the evidence is "substantially outweighed by the danger of unfair prejudice," then it doesn't get in. The police weren't on trial for wrongfully convicting Avery back in 1985; he was, for murdering Teresa Halbach. The jury might get off track if the defense was permitted to harp on the details of the wrongful conviction and decide the case for the wrong reasons. I could almost hear Kratz summing up the State's argument: "The objective of a jury trial is to find the truth, Judge, not to muddy the waters."

But where the prosecution would see prejudice and confusion of the issues, Avery's lawyers would see critical evidence necessary for the defense. I imagined how effectively Dean Strang might argue the point. He'd point out that a police conspiracy was the cornerstone of the defense, and however fantastic it might appear to some, the defendant had marshaled some credible evidence in support of his claim. "Remember, Your Honor," he would implore the Court, "Mr. Avery is charged with a crime that could deprive him of his liberty for the rest of his life. He must be allowed to present his defense!"

But as it turned out, my musings about the rules of evidence were unnecessary and my fear was misplaced, because a few months later, Judge Willis issued a well-reasoned and firm decision. Why did I doubt? The fact that the defendant was wrongfully convicted of first degree sexual assault and attempted murder in 1985 would get in, as would the fact that he had a thirty-six million dollar lawsuit pending against the County. But that's as far as it would go. There'd be no mention of the details of the wrongful conviction – nothing about a suspiciously created composite drawing or about an affidavit hidden in the Sheriff's safe. The jury wouldn't know about Gregory Allen's sexual psychopathic conduct leading up to his attack of Penny Beerntsen or about his shenanigans on the beach two summers earlier. Nor would they hear about Denis Vogel's inaccurate claim that Allen's probation agent said he had an airtight alibi.

I was hugely relieved. Without its details, the conspiracy theory lost most of its punch. The connection between the defendant's wrongful conviction and the murder prosecution would strike the jury as mere speculation, and the spotlight would be where it belongs, I thought, on Steven Avery, the accused murderer.

THIRTY-ONE

IT WAS THE most dramatic turn of events since Jerry Buting found the unsecured blood vial in the Clerk of Courts office. Ken Kratz made the announcement at a press conference carried live on TV. His words were unlikely to reach the tender ears of children since they were broadcast in the early afternoon during soap opera hours, but it didn't matter to Kratz. Ever the advocate for the kids, Ken had a warning for the viewers. What followed would be graphic, he warned, you parents might want to have the kids leave the room, or at the very least, cover their ears.

The details couldn't have been more horrid, and Kratz didn't hold back.

Police had long suspected that Steve's sixteen-year-old nephew, Brendan Dassey, had accompanied his uncle in Teresa's murder. And now, as cops and prosecutors refer to defendants' confessions, Dassey had puked all over himself.

Brendan said something in a recent police interview that caught the attention of one of the investigators. "We

248

believed he knew more than he was telling us," Calumet County Sheriff Jerry Pagel later said at the news conference. So they interviewed him again, and this time Brendan confessed to participating with his uncle in Teresa's rape and murder.

It was the stuff of a cheaply made horror film – it even happened on Halloween – except it was true. Sparing none of the gruesome details, Kratz recounted the events as Brendan described them to the investigator, one step at a time.

Brendan got off the school bus at the usual time, about 3:45, and found a letter for his Uncle Steve in the mailbox. As he walked up to Steve's trailer, he heard a female voice inside screaming, "Help me!"

When he answered the door, Steve was "covered in sweat." He invited Brendan inside and asked him if he wanted to "get some of that stuff," pointing to the bedroom. Brendan walked in and saw Teresa Halbach naked and bound face up on the bed with handcuffs and leg irons.

Steve told him he already raped Teresa and wanted to continue, encouraging him to join in. Teresa cried and pleaded with him, begging him not to do it, to let her go, and to get his uncle to stop. But instead, Brendan got on top of her and raped her for about five minutes while Steve watched from the side.

After that it got even worse. The two of them went into the living room and watched TV for 10 to 15 minutes. "That's how you do it," Steve said, telling Brendan he was proud of him. While the TV played, Steve talked about killing Teresa and burning her body. He returned from the kitchen a few minutes later carrying a knife with a six- to eight-inch blade. Then they returned to the bedroom, where Steve told Teresa he was going to kill her. He stabbed her in the stomach and handed the knife to Brendan and told him to cut her throat. Brendan obeyed, and Steve told him to cut off some of her hair.

Brendan did that too. Then Steve went over to Teresa and strangled her.

They took off the shackles and tied her with a rope and took her to the garage where even though Brendan believed she was already dead, Steve shot her about 10 times with a rifle, including a few times on the left side of her head. He and Steve threw Teresa's body onto a fire pit that was already burning when Brendan came home from school. They put tires and brush on top to accelerate the fire, and while Teresa's body burned, they drove her RAV4 to the edge of the Salvage Yard and hid it from view. Steve returned to the fire pit a few days later and broke up some of Teresa's remaining bones with a shovel, and he then buried them in areas scattered around the premises.

Kratz concluded his remarks by telling the viewers that Brendan admitted that he should have done something to stop his uncle Steve, but he forced him to do it and threatened to stab him if he told anyone. When one of the detectives asked why he participated, Brendan replied, "I wanted to see how it felt ... sex."

* * *

The gruesome details of Brendan Dassey's confession shocked the public and even changed the views of some of the most conspiracy-minded people in town, convincing them that their former hero was guilty after all. But for those with an unshakable conviction that the police were corrupt, his confession only solidified their views. If what he said was true, they reasoned, there'd be blood all over the place – especially in Steve's bedroom where the victim was supposedly stabbed. But the police didn't find any blood in the bedroom – not even a drop – though they eventually found a bullet fragment in the garage. All this butchery and not one drop of Teresa's blood in the bedroom – how could that be? The cops must have psychologically tortured Brendan until he made it up, he's barely seventeen, after all, and rumor has it he's slow.

As for me, I felt much better about the prospects for a conviction after Dassey's confession. Kratz added charges of first-degree sexual assault, kidnapping, and false imprisonment to the murder and mutilation charges. Avery faced life imprisonment plus 128 years if he was convicted of all the charges. *That ought to do*, I thought.

But there was another part of me that felt like the system had failed, and I wondered if we should have seen it coming. I was familiar with the direction of Steven Avery's life in the months leading up to Teresa's murder, and the trajectory wasn't a good one.

It's almost universal. Despite their initial idealism, most people who work in the criminal justice system develop an edge of cynicism after awhile – seen too many repeat offenders, I guess. So it wasn't surprising that from the moment Steven Avery walked out of prison, the courthouse crowd started taking bets on when he would be back in. They knew what he was like before he went to prison, and if they didn't, one of the old-timers filled them in. The cat burning incident, the threats to burn down his parent's house, the crimes of domestic violence against his fiancée, ramming into the wife of a deputy's car and accosting her at gunpoint – these incidents became part of courthouse lore, and they still resided in the long-term institutional memory of the local justice system when Avery was exonerated and released from prison.

And he had another strike against him, one not shared by most former-offenders trying to stitch their lives back together after serving their time. Because his conviction and sentence had been vacated, when he walked out of prison he wasn't placed on parole. That meant no supervision, no counseling, no weekly meetings with a parole agent to keep tabs on him, and no support.

So the joy of freedom faded after awhile and things started taking a turn for the worse. While he beat the predictions of the most pessimistic of the courthouse prognosticators, it wasn't long until the "innocent man" had a few brushes with the law.

The first one was just a speeding ticket. The officer clocked him at seventy-nine in a fifty-five mile-per-hour zone. The rookie ADA handling the case must have figured the County owed him one, because he amended the ticket to defective speedometer and Avery promptly paid the fine.

Then it got more serious. Avery had taken up with a similarly lost soul by the name of Carla Schwartz. They met at a convenience store and apparently it was love at first sight. But the honeymoon didn't last long because a few months later, Carla had to call the police. She had moved in with Avery, and one weekend when he was up north, he found out she was out at the races and she hadn't let him know she was going out. When Carla came home a little after 11:00, she and Avery got into an argument. She told him "to pack his shit up and move out," at which point he pushed her, causing her to fall into a chair and hit her head. Avery got on top of her and started hitting her, telling her he should kill her. Carla got up to call 911, but before she could talk to the dispatcher, Avery ripped the phone out of the wall and began choking her to the point where she lost consciousness. When she came to, he dragged her out to the car by her arms and said, "I should get the gun and kill you."

In light of the conflict of interest stemming from Avery's wrongful conviction lawsuit, Mark farmed out the case to a local attorney who agreed to serve as a special prosecutor. Due to discrepancies between Carla Schwartz's original version of the events and what she told the officer a few days later, as well as her request to drop the charges, the special prosecutor directed the police to issue a disorderly conduct citation instead of issuing criminal charges. Somehow the media never got wind of it, and as far as the public was concerned, Steven Avery was still a hero.

There was also some evidence that Avery was trying to warn the world that he was in trouble and that his life was heading dangerously downhill. In an interview with the *Milwaukee Journal Sentinel*, he described how he was often depressed and full of frustration and anger.

"Sometimes it'll last all day," he said. "That's when I try to stay away from everybody."

"Sometimes I cuss them out, sometimes I just go for a ride – it ain't nothing to put on a hundred miles."

He confided that he cries sometimes because his twin boys didn't want anything to do with him, and "there's probably too much going on inside my head – brain can't put it all in."

He complained about the State not providing him with counseling or other help in the transition – "they just let you out the door." But he also admitted that he would have refused to see a psychiatrist even if one was offered. "I can't tell him my problem. I'll sort it out myself," he said. "What can he do that I can't?"

He gave assurances that he didn't really want to return to prison, but when he reflected about how he used to sit on a picnic bench in the prison yard and count the jets that flew by, his words didn't sound very convincing: "Sometimes," he said, "I feel like it's easier in there. Some days, just put me back there, get it all over with."

* * *

As the trial date approached, I thought the chances of a conviction were better than even. But better than even isn't good enough for the prosecution; the evidence should be overwhelming. So I was still a basket case on the eve of the trial. The quirky circumstances of the investigation scared me – especially how Colborn and Lenk found the keys.

If only Kratz could get Dassey's confession in front of the jury, I thought, the defense wouldn't stand a chance. But given Dassey's Fifth Amendment right against self-incrimination, the State couldn't force him to take the stand.

There was one more option, though. It strikes some as unseemly, but we do it all the time. We use little fish to get bigger fish by cutting them a deal. Kratz could offer Dassey a plea agreement in return for his testimony against his uncle Steve, maybe a reduction in the charges, or more likely, an agreement to recommend a parole eligibility date that would get him out of prison say, when he was fifty years old.

But getting Dassey to accept a plea agreement wouldn't be easy. The close knit Avery clan is fiercely loyal to each other, and Allan Avery would undoubtedly pressure his grandson not to cut a deal and testify against Steve. Also, Kratz had to be careful. You don't offer much lenience to a cold-blooded killer, even if he's a seventeen year-old boy with diminished mental capacities whose role model is Steven Avery. So I wasn't surprised when in the end the parties failed to strike a deal, and I knew that without Dassey's confession the outcome of the trial was far from clear.

THIRTY-TWO

S TEVEN AVERY'S TRIAL – this time for murder – was set to begin on February 5, 2007. The astonishing twists and turns of the past eighteen months were about to culminate in a fascinating six-week trial. The Green Bay and Milwaukee TV stations had decided weeks earlier how they would cover the proceedings. Key moments, like the opening statements and closing arguments, would be broadcast live, while the rest of the trial would be available on-line, and all six stations would cover the lawyer's daily press conferences on their evening news shows. The local newspaper started running daily stories. "Defense Gearing up to Argue Blood was Planted," read one of the headlines in the *Manitowoc Herald Times Reporter.*

No one in the public outside law enforcement and the court system knew at the time, but on the night before the trial began, and a few days after the *Herald Times* reported that the defense would be allowed to present evidence of the wrongful conviction lawsuit and the blood vial, former Chief Inspector

Gene Kusche died unexpectedly, sitting in his favorite living room chair in the comfort of his home. The official cause of death was listed as acute myocardial infarction – a heart attack – and although friends said Gene wasn't a religious man, he had a bible at his side.

Gene had obviously been in denial. I ran into him a few weeks before he died in the courthouse parking lot where we spoke briefly about the Avery case in the midst of television trucks with their live feeds and monstrous antenna rising thirty feet high into the sky. It was a shame Avery was released from prison, he said with a straight face, because Allen and Avery could have both assaulted Penny Beerntsen on the beach that day. The not so subtle inference: *If we hadn't cut him loose, Teresa Halbach would still be alive.*

Kusche had expressed similar doubts at his deposition in the wrongful conviction lawsuit a few months earlier. "Yes," he replied to one of the plaintiff's attorneys, "I've heard that DNA evidence supposedly exonerated Mr. Avery, but I don't know that on personal knowledge because I haven't seen the reports. I don't believe everything I read in the newspapers."

"Who knows," he suggested, "maybe the DNA evidence was fabricated. Or maybe they both did it."

Admittedly, it's mostly speculation, but did Gene Kusche's death have anything to do with the fact that the Avery trial would start the next day? The headline in the local paper the night before he died covered the judge's decision to allow the jury to hear the blood vial and wrongful conviction evidence. Was Gene afraid that Avery would walk for Teresa's murder? Or was his death just another odd coincidence in a case that was chock full of odd coincidences from the very beginning?

* * *

Judge Willis is no Lance Ito – in fact, he's just the opposite. Despite its complexity, he was determined that the trial would be concluded in six weeks or less. But given the amount of pretrial publicity, as well as the strongly held views of some on the panel, it took a full week to select the jury. By week's end, though, the hundred and forty-four prospects on the panel had been winnowed down to the chosen sixteen – eight women and eight men, two of whom would serve as alternates.

The first day of trial finally arrived. Kratz delivered a three hour opening statement that, if predictable, was also compelling. Using power point photographs and high-tech schematic drawings, he drew a picture in the jurors' minds of the Avery Salvage Yard with its cluster of trailer homes and outbuildings, which served as the offices, garages, and living quarters for the family. And speaking in his pleasant low-key comforting way, he laid out a convincing account of Avery's guilt, and the jurors, especially the older ones, took to him immediately. *I promise*, he assured them, *by the end of this case you will have no doubt who murdered Teresa Halbach.*

Dean Strang hit a home run for the defense. With his sincere and thoughtful demeanor, he asked the jurors not to prejudge his client's guilt. Once they heard all the facts, he told them, they would have serious doubts about the State's evidence, including how the victim's keys got into Avery's bedroom and how his blood got into her car. He said the Sheriff's Department focused almost entirely on the defendant in the investigation because of their disdain for him, calling their technique "tunnel vision." "The police didn't kill Teresa Halbach," he said, "they have that in common with Steven Avery; but they wanted to believe he did." He told the jurors he was going to ask them at the end of the case "to get it right this time."

Kratz and the rest of the prosecution team started presenting their case the next day. With Tom Fallon from the AG's office and nationally known DNA guru Norm Gahn from the Milwaukee County DA's office assisting, he began by laying out a timeline leading up to Teresa's death, with phone calls and a paper trail detailing her whereabouts on Halloween 2005.

They presented a steady stream of physical evidence, starting with the human remains and some blue jean rivets found inside the fire pit outside Steven Avery's trailer. The rivets came from a pair of Daisy Fuentes jeans similar to a pair owned by Teresa Halbach, and the bone fragments included a skull section that remained intact enough for an expert to determine that the deceased had been shot twice in the head – just like Brendan Dassey had said.

Sherry Culhane, still a DNA analyst at the Wisconsin Crime Lab, and testifying in yet another case involving Steven Avery, said the chances were one in a billion that the teeth and bone fragments found in the fire pit did not belong to Teresa Halbach. She also tested the blood stains lifted from Teresa's car, and they matched Avery's DNA profile, as did some skin fragments on Teresa's keys.

Jerry Buting turned the State's presentation of the physical evidence upside down by suggesting in one blistering cross-examination after another that the evidence was planted. Playing the bad cop, he attacked the investigating officers for what he perceived as their lack of caution in following procedure. He questioned how four police officers failed to find a bullet fragment containing Teresa Halbach's DNA that a Manitowoc County detective allegedly discovered a few months later in Avery's garage, terming it "the magic bullet."

"Did you see a bullet on November 6?" he asked one of the officers from Calumet County, who swiftly responded in the negative.

"Because if you had, you would have collected it, right?" Buting asked rhetorically, "because it would have been an extremely important piece of evidence, right?"

"There were four of you in that garage, and not one of you found a bullet or a bullet fragment!"

"Correct," the officer replied sheepishly.

And Buting pulled no punches when he challenged how Teresa's car keys ended up in Avery's bedroom, all but indicting Colborn and Lenk for planting them there. It turns out the bedroom was searched six times, not just three, like I thought, before the two Manitowoc County officers found the keys "in plain sight" right in front of them, according to Buting.

Kratz tried to soften the blow by suggesting the keys weren't discovered earlier because the initial searches of the expansive buildings on the Avery property, including Steve's trailer, were cursory sweeps and not detailed examinations. But the explanation rang hollow to many.

He also called a Calumet County deputy who was in the bedroom with Lenk and Colborn, for at least part of the time. "Based upon your positioning a couple feet away from that key, did you believe that either Lenk or Colborn had an opportunity, out of your eyesight, to place, or what's called plant, that key there?" Kratz asked.

"No, they did not," the officer replied.

But on cross-examination, Buting beat up on him and the deputy had to retreat: "My actual observations, I would have to say that it could be possible, as in I was doing other things, I was taking photographs, I was searching the nightstand."

A TV reporter interviewed Allan Avery outside the courthouse a few days into the trial.

"We're sick and tired of them saying bones were found on Avery's Auto Salvage," Allan said. "They found nothing. All they found is somebody put a car there."

"Brendan Dassey is innocent and my son is innocent," he continued. "If you start from the beginning, they plugged the highway off and kicked us out of our houses for eight days so they could plant evidence. This is not right. We need to give our justice system a good goin' over."

Kratz called Bobby Dassey, Brendan's older brother, the following day. Bobby testified that he saw a girl walking toward his Uncle Steve's trailer at 2:45 p.m. on Halloween day. He also said a few days after Teresa Halbach went missing, his uncle jokingly asked him if he wanted to help hide a body, and then he kidded that she probably went to Mexico.

Brendan and Bobby's brother, Blaine, also testified, telling the jury he saw a huge bonfire burning when he returned from trick-or-treating the night Teresa disappeared. He said he saw someone near the fire but claimed he couldn't remember who it was.

But as they neared the end of their case, the prosecution still hadn't dealt effectively with the blood vial defense. They hoped the jury would instinctively see through the preposterous claim, but they needed something more than just hope. They needed proof – hard, objective, undeniable proof.

So they turned to science.

Chemists add a chemical compound called ethylenediamine-tetraacetic acid, EDTA for short, when they test a blood specimen for DNA so that the specimen doesn't degrade. In its natural form blood doesn't contain EDTA, so you wouldn't expect to find any, not even a trace, in the blood stains lifted from Teresa's car – unless, of course, it was planted.

Judge Willis had already granted the State's motion to test the blood stains for EDTA, but it wasn't clear whether a sufficiently reliable test existed. So with the assistance of the US Attorney's office, Kratz contacted the FBI and enlisted their help.

Dr. Marc Lebeau, head of the FBI's chemical analysis unit, dropped everything, and working round the clock for two weeks, he and his colleagues developed a new protocol. As the prosecution expected, Lebeau's analysis indicated that while the specimen of Avery's blood in the vial from the Clerk's office contained EDTA, the blood stains lifted from the RAV4 did not. If Judge Willis found the test sufficiently reliable, Dr. Lebeau could testify and end the nonsense of the blood vial defense once and for all.

The next day Kratz told the Court he wanted to put Lebeau on the stand.

It would be one of the most crucial decisions Judge Willis would make, and it might well determine the outcome of the trial. Noting that the defense knew about the blood vial before the State did and they could have pursued testing themselves, Judge Willis sided with the State. Dr. Lebeau could take the stand.

With his curriculum vitae and the EDTA results in hand, the State's newfound star witness walked up to the witness stand, took the oath, and then waited for a gloating Ken Kratz to start his examination. He explained to the jury how he and his colleagues used blind testing to make sure their protocol was valid before they tested the two specimens. The results of the tests showed that the blood in the vial contained EDTA, but the blood stains lifted from the RAV4 did not. It was safe to assume, Lebeau said, that the blood inside Teresa Halbach's car did not come from the vial.

Buting established during cross-examination that EDTA testing was last done during the O.J. Simpson trial, and the testing in that case drew criticism because scientists discovered errors in the protocol during the trial. During a news conference later that night, he harshly criticized the EDTA testing as "voodoo science", and Dean Strang likened it to "palm reading" and "astrology."

But the damage was done and the defense was completely deflated. With the blood vial defense discredited, the other claims of evidence planting would lose their credibility too, and the entire conspiracy theory would collapse. They had to act fast.

They must have had their witness waiting in the wings because the next day, the defense opened up with testimony from Janine Arvizu, a laboratory quality control auditor, who questioned the accuracy of Dr. Lebeau's test results. Arvizu said the FBI's hastily developed testing protocol wasn't designed to rule out the presence of EDTA in the bloodstains because the limits of the analysis machine weren't low enough to find it in such a small amount of blood.

"The fact that EDTA was not detected in the stains does not mean EDTA was not in the stains," she said. "It certainly is quite plausible that the blood stains swabbed from the RAV4 contained EDTA, but the lab simply was not able to detect it."

The defense rested the following Monday without calling Avery to the stand. When Judge Willis asked him outside the presence of the jury whether he wanted to testify, he replied he was innocent so why should he. With the blood vial defense on the ropes and Avery deciding not to testify, I thought his chance for an acquittal had withered away. At least, that's what I had hoped at the time.

'* * *

With much of the public tuning in by television or on-line, the jury listened attentively as the lawyers presented their closing arguments.

Six weeks earlier in his opening statement Kratz told the jurors he was showing them the cover of a jigsaw puzzle; now, addressing them at the end of the trial, he said he would help them put the pieces together. He spoke of "the clues and the secrets" found in Teresa Halbach's car and inside Steven Avery's trailer. "Teresa, by her DNA and where it was found, is telling you a story," he said. "She's telling you 'this is where I was,' she's telling you 'this is what happened to me,' and she's telling you 'this is how I was killed.'"

Ken was extremely effective, and he has reason to be proud.

"Cases are decided on facts, at least from the State's perspective," he said, taking a not-so-subtle dig at the defense.

"You know, the funny thing about facts is: facts are stubborn. Facts don't change. You can twist them, you can beat 'em up, you can try to massage, if you will, the facts. But facts don't change."

Jerry Buting and Dean Strang shared duties in presenting the closing argument for the defense. Continuing their good cop/bad cop routine, with Buting hammering home the police conspiracy theory and Strang reflecting more broadly about burdens of proof and the meaning of beyond a reasonable doubt.

Buting argued there was plenty of evidence alright, but it all pointed to a frame-up by the police. "Let me make one thing very clear right here at the outset," he said, "we do not and have never claimed the police killed Teresa Halbach, and at least in that respect, they have something in common with Steven Avery. However, the person or persons who did kill

263

Teresa knew exactly who the police would want to blame for this crime."

He reminded the jury that Manitowoc County sheriff's deputies were guarding Teresa's car for the first four hours after it was found and suggested the police could have taken Avery's blood from the vial at the Clerk's office after normal working hours and then planted some in her car. Yet, investigators did not find the defendant's fingerprints in the victim's car, he said, "because fingerprints are very difficult to plant."

The shrill tone and sarcasm in his voice reached fever pitch when he addressed the circumstances of Colborn and Lenk's discovery of Teresa's keys in Avery's bedroom.

"Lenk gets up, walks out the door, comes back a minute later and, oh, my gosh, lo and behold in plain view, look at this key. This magic key that no one ever finds before suddenly appears in plain view."

Steven Avery in court

THIRTY-THREE

JUDGE WILLIS INSTRUCTED the Clerk to spin the tumbler. After five weeks of testimony from nearly 60 witnesses, almost 500 court exhibits, and a day and a half of closing arguments, it was finally time for the jury to decide. Sixteen jurors were seated at the beginning of the trial and now it was time to eliminate four of them. The Clerk spun the tumbler and read off the names, and the four alternates stood up and silently left the courtroom. It was down to the twelve, six women and six men, who would decide.

The jury began deliberating at 12:54 in the afternoon and retired at six that evening without reaching a verdict. But they had to pick a foreperson and wade through pages of complicated jury instructions, so the lack of a verdict that night wasn't a surprise. *They want to be careful*, I told myself, *a man's life is in their hands*.

I went home that night confident that the jury would see through the now-discredited conspiracy theory and swiftly return a guilty verdict the next day, probably in the morning.

Now that the prosecution had shown the blood vial defense for what it was, a desperate attempt to shift blame, I couldn't imagine how they could do otherwise. Other than the happenstance of Lenk and Colborn finding the key, the defense had presented little of substance, and in light of all the rest of the evidence, even that seemed fairly harmless now. For more than a year, Buting and Strang had shouted "police conspiracy" to anyone with ears, but now I assumed the jurors had heard enough conjecture and were ready to decide.

But I shouldn't have been so confident. The jury resumed at nine the next morning, and after several more hours of deliberating without reaching a verdict, they sent Judge Willis a note – the jury wanted a magnifying glass, that's right, a magnifying glass.

Prosecutors squirm when deliberating jurors make a request or have a question they want answered by the judge because it usually means they're having serious doubts about the State's case. *Why did they want a magnifying glass,* I asked myself. *Was it to inspect the photograph of the RAV4? Were they buying the defense that the blood was planted and asked for a magnifying glass so they could take a look for themselves?*

It was impossible to say, but Judge Willis gathered the parties and brought in the jury. They are not to conduct their own investigation, the Judge told them, they are to base their decision on the evidence in the record, and nothing more.

The jury resumed deliberating a few minutes later and then retired at six that evening. Still, no verdict. They'd sat stone-faced through five weeks of testimony and there was no way of knowing which way they were leaning. It had me on edge, and I could only imagine how Kratz and the rest of the prosecution team felt – not to mention the Halbachs.

It wasn't long after the jurors began deliberating the next morning when they sent an even more distressing note to

266

Judge Willis. They wanted to review the testimony from Sherry Culhane, and worse, they only wanted her cross-examination.

Now I was really worried.

Jerry Buting had established two things during his cross-examination of crime lab analyst Culhane, which I assumed were now on the minds of the jurors. First, Steven Avery's DNA was not found on the trigger of the rifle that he allegedly used to shoot Teresa Halbach. And second, there was no blood on the rifle's barrel.

"The victim in this case was shot at close range, wasn't she?" Buting had asked.

"And you would typically find blood spatter on a rifle barrel that was used to shoot someone at close range, wouldn't you?"

"Yet when you examined the rifle that my client allegedly used to shoot the victim in this case, you didn't observe any blood spatter, isn't that right?"

Buting's assumptions weren't valid. A gunshot at close range doesn't always leave blood spatter, and the absence of the shooter's DNA on the trigger wasn't unusual. But thanks to CSI and other popular TV crime shows, jurors assume there's always physical evidence left at crime scenes, and now they almost insist on proof by DNA. Sherry Culhane had appropriately qualified her answers, but it didn't matter, Buting had sewn doubt in the minds of some of the jurors.

Judge Willis called in the lawyers again, and after some prodding, the parties agreed that the fairest way to handle the jury's request was to read all of Culhane's testimony concerning the rifle, not just her cross-examination by Buting. So the Clerk called in the jury and Judge Willis read the testimony out loud in its entirety. After deliberating a few more hours, the jury retired for the evening. Two and a half days. Still, no verdict.

I fell asleep that night thinking about Teresa Halbach's parents. They'd sat stoically through the entire trial, expressing quiet confidence in the system that they hoped would bring justice to the man who murdered their daughter. No parent of a murdered child expects closure, but a guilty verdict would at least end the drawn-out legal proceedings against Teresa's killer. I thought how an acquittal would devastate them, how it would add insult to an injury that you'd think could be insulted no further. I knew that if anyone could handle such pain, it would be the Halbach family with their unshakable faith. But at the same time, I thought, hadn't they already suffered enough?

* * *

It was just after four-thirty the following day when the bailiff made the announcement. After deliberating for three days, the jury had reached a verdict. The parties and a sizeable crowd assembled, and when everyone was in place, the Clerk called in the jurors. They filed into the courtroom with their heads down – not a good sign for Avery, I thought hopefully.

"Has the Jury reached a verdict?" Judge Willis asked in a calm but firm tone of voice.

"Yes, Your Honor," the foreperson replied.

"Please hand the verdict forms to the bailiff."

The bailiff handed over the forms while the courtroom itself seemed to wait in silence. The Judge had previously warned the spectators against outbursts, and after slowly reading through the forms, he announced the verdicts.

"As to the charge of Party to the Crime of First Degree Intentional Homicide as charged in count one of the Information, we the jury find the defendant, Steven A. Avery, guilty."

A sigh of relief swept through the courtroom, except for behind the defense table, where the Avery family was as shocked and devastated as the Halbachs were relieved. Judge Willis mercifully wrapped it up by announcing that the jury had also found the defendant guilty of being a felon in possession of a firearm, but not guilty of mutilating a corpse.

The sexual assault and false imprisonment charges were previously dismissed since they couldn't be proved without Brendan Dassey's testimony. But none of that mattered. With his conviction for murder, Steven Avery would never again see the light of day.

* * *

Teresa Halbach never imagined that a video diary she made three years before she died would be played during a sentencing hearing for the man convicted of her murder. The voice and face of a beautiful, grace-filled, loving, and very much alive young woman filled the courtroom as Teresa told us how she loved hugs, her family, God, making people laugh, traveling, people giving her compliments, and music groups like the Beatles and No Doubt.

"I love knowing that I like who I am," she said. "I love taking pictures. I love holding a camera in my hand. I love kids. I love babies. I don't hate anyone. I love a lot of people. I feel loved."

"Let's say I died tomorrow," Teresa said into the camera. "I don't think I will. I think I have a lot more to do. I just want people I love to know that whenever I die, that I was happy. That I'm happy with what I did with my life."

Her family sobbed as Teresa's voice filled the courtroom.

She said if she dies early she wished she could have been a mother "because that's the one thing I've always known that I want to be – a mom. And I will be a good mom one day. I will. As long as I'm happy," she said with a smile.

We don't have the death penalty in Wisconsin, but if we did, Steven Avery probably would have been executed – at least that's what the prosecution would likely have sought. Instead of death, life imprisonment without the possibility of parole is the maximum penalty for murder in Wisconsin. Judge Willis could set a parole eligibility date that would allow Avery's release some day, say when he was ninety if he happened to live that long. But with a crime as deplorable as this one, nobody expected him to do so, and the Judge didn't prove them wrong.

With the sentence nearly a foregone conclusion, there wasn't much to argue about, but the lawyers, being lawyers, argued anyhow.

Kratz briefly commented on the defendant's criminal history, including the cat burning incident, and then he recounted some of the most diabolical details of his most recent crime.

Strang said he didn't know what happened the day Teresa was murdered, but he believes in Steven Avery. "There's more good in this man than there is bad," he said.

When it was his turn to speak, Steven Avery said he felt sorry for Teresa Halbach's family and their friends, as well as his family and himself. "It's hurting everybody," he said unconvincingly. He also said he would prove his innocence some day – just like the last time.

"Teresa Halbach, I didn't kill," he said. "I'm innocent for all of this, and I figure later on I'll prove myself innocent. I feel bad about it. I wish they'd catch the guy who did it, whoever did it, because I didn't do it, honest to God."

And then it was time for Judge Willis to hand down the sentence. After noting that he had committed a calculated premeditated murder, he addressed the defendant directly.

"You are probably the most dangerous individual ever to set foot in this courtroom," he told Avery. "From what I see, nothing in your life suggests that society would ever be safe from your behavior."

And then he sentenced him to life imprisonment, without the possibility of parole.

* * *

On the morning of June 4, 2007, twenty-one years after passing through them the first time and less than four years after walking out a free man, Steven Avery was escorted through the gates at Dodge Correctional Institute in Waupun. There were no smiles this time, no cameras, no klieg lights, and no pretty reporters asking for a moment of his time. The doors clanged shut, and for the rest of his life, barring any more shocking revelations concerning the murder of Teresa Halbach, the nation's most famous exoneree will unceremoniously be known as Wisconsin State Prison Inmate Number 00122987.

EPILOGUE

A few weeks after Steven Avery was sentenced, Jody and the kids and I drove up to Neshotah Beach on the north side of Two Rivers. Summer returned early to Wisconsin that year, and thanks to an early season warm front temperatures had risen, preposterously, into the lower nineties. We popped open an umbrella and spread out a blanket in the sand while the girls splashed around in the fifty degree water and the boys rode the waves into shore.

Call it obsession, but I wanted to see if the poplar tree was still there – the place where twenty-two years earlier Gregory Allen lay in waiting for his prey. So my son Tom and I started jogging north along the beach, making our way out of the park and into the wilderness, where fifty yards inland the towering pines still kept watch over what was happening below.

We approached First Creek a mile into our run, where Allen had lunged out from the poplar tree and manhandled Penny Beerntsen over the dunes. But the tree wasn't there. A few measly shrubs struggled for survival ten feet from the shore, but they were far too small to have spent the last twenty-two years growing. Maybe high waves from a storm had washed it away.

But, in truth, I was glad it was gone. An injustice perpetrated upon the local court system had persisted for twenty-two years. Festering like a cancer, it let an uncharged assailant repeat his crime, this time in Green Bay, it temporarily turned Penny Beerntsen's life upside down, though Penny soon recovered and is now a major voice for criminal justice reform, and it turned Steven Avery into an even more dangerous monster than he was when he was sent to prison the first time. And when two highly skilled defense attorneys resurrected that injustice twenty years later to defend him in a murder trial, it nearly destroyed the local justice system and let a madman go free. But Avery's conviction destroyed the injustice once and for all, and if the waters of Lake Michigan had washed away another sign of the original crime, so much the better.

I'd worked up a pretty good sweat by the time Tom and I got back to the park, so I ran down the beach with a full head of steam and after a clumsy version of high-stepping over the waves, I dove into the water. When I opened my eyes and looked at the rippled sand on the bottom, all I saw was sunlight and water. I ran out as fast as I ran in and rejoined Jody, looking beautiful as always under the umbrella. "Did you hear sweetie," I said, with my heart still pounding, "they're talking about putting the glass back on the dome."

* * *

Since 1989, more than two hundred fifty wrongfully convicted persons have been exonerated by DNA testing in the United States. Seventeen of them served time on death row

273

before their convictions were overturned. The problem was so widespread in Illinois that in 2000, Governor George Ryan, noting that 13 death row inmates had been exonerated since the mid-seventies when capital punishment was reinstated there, placed a moratorium on capital punishment in that state.

It's impossible to know how many other wrongful convictions remain undetected since many criminal convictions are secured without physical evidence, leaving nothing left behind to be tested for DNA. Even when physical evidence is obtained, the evidence is frequently no longer available once the appeal period has lapsed. In fact, nearly one quarter of cases closed by the Innocence Project since 2004 were closed because of lost or missing evidence.

How many wrongful convictions are caused by official misconduct? No doubt, honest mistakes account for many of them, but the Innocence Project estimates that police and/or prosecutorial misconduct were factors in thirty-seven of the first seventy-four exonerations uncovered by DNA. The list of misconduct includes deliberate suggestiveness in identification procedures; mishandling, mistreatment or destruction of evidence; withholding of evidence from the defense; coercion of false confessions; and the use of unreliable government informants. Inexcusably, prosecutors whose misconduct factored into wrongful convictions almost always go unpunished and often even advance in their careers.

In response to the recent spate of high-profile exonerations, including Steven Avery's, the American Bar Association amended its *Model Rules of Professional Conduct* to include a section entitled, "Special Responsibilities of a Prosecutor." Reminding prosecutors that they have "the responsibility of a minister of justice, and not simply that of an advocate," the model rule provides that if a prosecutor knows of clear and convincing evidence that a convicted person is innocent, he or she must promptly seek to remedy the conviction by disclosing the evidence to the defendant and to the court.

This sounds like common sense, but if the Avery case tells us anything, it isn't necessarily so.

Observers in and outside the criminal justice system are acutely aware of the problem of wrongful convictions and are earnestly looking for answers. In the last few years, Wisconsin, New Jersey, North Carolina, and several large city police departments throughout the country have implemented new procedures that have proven successful in improving the accuracy of eye-witness identifications. In Wisconsin, the Avery Task Force inspired legislation that requires every police agency in the state to adopt guidelines on identification procedures that address issues such as proper instructions to witnesses, double-blind testing, and sequential presentation of suspects in line-ups or photographs in arrays. The legislation also clarifies which laboratories in the state are responsible for post-conviction DNA testing and requires that testing that might prove innocence be given priority.

But while procedural safeguards may help, they still don't get to the root of the problem. Larger issues are at stake, such as the way we select prosecutors. Whether elected, as they are in most states, or appointed, as in the federal system, the office of prosecuting attorney is fraught with political pressure. The media and the politically driven "tough on crime" mentality of many in the public produce ever stricter crime legislation, which makes it difficult for even well-meaning prosecutors to make decisions based only upon reasoned judgment and sound discretion. The same holds true for judges, who face similar pressures in handing down sentences.

There are things that could be done to change the knee-jerk "tough on crime" mentality of some prosecutors. DA conferences could include a presentation about our unique role in the justice system. Changing the way prosecutors are selected is a more drastic solution, but it's at least worth exploring. And there are others.

But it's impossible to entirely preclude the politics of crime from influencing the decisions of prosecutors and judges. After all, they must either face the electorate at the polls or serve at the whim of the politician who appointed them.

So what's the solution?

Addressing a roomful of federal prosecutors in Washington D.C. in 1940, United States Attorney General Robert H. Jackson began by defining the nature of the problem:

> It would probably be within the range of that exaggeration permitted in Washington to say that assembled in this room is one of the most powerful peace-time forces known to our country. The prosecutor has more control over life, liberty, and reputation than any other person in America. His discretion is tremendous. He can have citizens investigated, and if he is that kind of person, he can have this done to the tune of public sentiments and veiled or unveiled intimations. While the prosecutor at his best is one of the most beneficent forces in our society, when he acts from malice or other base motives, he is one of the worst.

And he closed by suggesting at least part of the solution:

> The qualities of a good prosecutor are as elusive and as impossible to define as those which mark a gentleman. And those who need to be told would not understand it anyway. A sensitiveness to fair play and sportsmanship is perhaps the best protection against the abuse of power, and the citizen's safety

lies in the prosecutor who tempers zeal with human kindness, who seeks truth and not victims, who serves the law and not factional purposes, and who approaches his task with humility.

Closer to home, as Penny Beerntsen put it in her testimony in Madison that day, some wrongful convictions are caused by the "moral shortcomings" of persons in power. None of us who work in the justice system is perfect, but as a court instruction characterizes jury duty, we have been "called upon to act in the most important affairs of life," so we must try our hardest to do what's right. Because if we don't, an injustice can fester for years.

Author's Note

The names of some persons portrayed in this book have been changed to protect their identity.

Eight months after Steven Avery's murder trial, 17-year-old Brendan Dassey was convicted and sentenced to life in prison for his role in the murder of Teresa Halbach. He will be eligible for parole in 2047 after serving 40 years of his sentence when he would be fifty-seven years old.

An independent investigation by the Wisconsin Attorney General concluded there was no intentional wrongdoing by the Sheriff or the District Attorney in Steven Avery's wrongful conviction, citing, instead, poor communication between law enforcement agencies. Any opinion expressed herein to the contrary is that of the author, and though shared by many, it is not shared by all.

The background photograph on the left side of the front cover shows the Manitowoc County Courthouse dome after its glass was shattered by a hail storm that swept through the city on June 28, 1950.

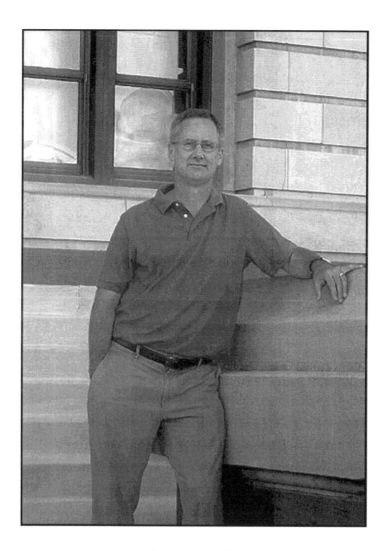

About the Author

Michael Griesbach is a prosecuting attorney in Manitowoc County, Wisconsin who played a significant role in some of the events described in this book. He hopes to leave readers better informed about the inner workings of the criminal justice system and more concerned about those whose lives it deeply affects.

Made in the USA
Charleston, SC
04 June 2011